Bound, an Earth Walker's Handbook

Bound, an Earth Walker's Handbook

Realm 666, New Canaan Edition

Charles S. Stone

RESOURCE *Publications* • Eugene, Oregon

BOUND, AN EARTH WALKER'S HANDBOOK
Realm 666, New Canaan Edition

Copyright © 2013 Charles S. Stone. All rights reserved. Except for brief quotations in critical publications or reviews, no part of this book may be reproduced in any manner without prior written permission from the publisher. Write: Permissions, Wipf and Stock Publishers, 199 W. 8th Ave., Suite 3, Eugene, OR 97401.

Unless otherwise indicated, all Scripture quotations are from The Holy Bible, New International Version®, NIV® Copyright © 1973, 1978, 1984, 2011, by Biblica, Inc.™ Used by permission. All rights reserved worldwide.

Artwork used by permission of David Braun, Middleburg, VA.

Resource Publications
An imprint of Wipf and Stock Publishers
199 W. 8th Ave., Suite 3
Eugene, OR 97401

www.wipfandstock.com

isbn 13: 978-1-62032-501-8

Manufactured in the U.S.A.

Contents

Foreword by Julia Overton | vii
Preface | xi
Abbreviations | xiii

Section 1   Introduction | 1
Section 2   Charging Charges | 5
Section 3   Stumbling Blocks | 22
Section 4   Wo|man: Nature & Nativity | 43
Section 5   Controvert | 69
Section 6   Finite Realm 666 | 95
Section 7   Appendices | 111

Appendix 1 | 111
Organizational Chart, 57th GSB

Appendix 2 | 112
Chain of Command, Delta Team, 5/57 GSG, 7th Holy Legion

Appendix 3 | 113
Mission Statement, Delta Team, 5/57 GSG

Appendix 4 | 114
Higher Organizational Mission Statements

Appendix 5 | 115
Standing Orders, Earth Walkers, 5/57 GSG

Appendix 6 | 115
Order of Battle, 6th Unholy Legion

Appendix 7 | 116
COTC Phases

Appendix 8 | 118
Charge Alarm Signals

Appendix 9 | 120
Calculating the Probability of Preservation

Appendix 10 | 122
AA Raphael's Spiritual Assessment Matrix (SPAM)

Appendix 11 | 123
Martial Prerequisites

Appendix 12 | 124
Media Prerequisites

Bibliography | 129

Foreword

CHARLIE STONE IS THE most flexible man I know. From a standing pike position he can put both palms flat on the floor and keep his legs perfectly straight . . . very unusual for a man. As I read *Bound* the same image comes to mind about his writing. He has taken several literary genres, bending, flexing, and shaping them together while keeping his message of religious and spiritual authenticity perfectly straight. He tells a story by identifying, in a fresh way, behaviors in the church that vex and embarrass some believers and send non-believers running for the hills instead of running to a community of believers, and he does so in a way that not only men, but also women, can relate to . . . also unusual for a man.

He does all this by creating an entire spiritual world outside planet Earth with angelic recruits who sign up for Corporeal Operative Training to intervene on behalf of the Descendants of Noah. Major Xhaliel, Team Leader of Delta Team, which operates in New Canaan (North America), gives the recruits his charge: "Among Guardians, Earth Walkers serve in the most demanding and dangerous role: covert, corporeal operations. Only the most capable of angels are selected to become Corporeal Operatives. . . . Merely understanding (let alone protecting) wo|mankind required all the abilities God gave me and it took me forever, pun intended, to acclimate to Finite Realm 666." And with this daunting backdrop, the recruits begin their journey toward an understanding of human kind.

This is a timeless message told in today's vocabulary. It conjures up images of the scariest video games but contains biting and truthful observations. On my own path to seminary, I cut my science fiction "eye teeth" on *Perelandra* and *That Hideous Strength* by C. S. Lewis. I entered Middle Earth and the battle of good and evil in Tolkein's trilogy—all written in the last century and beloved by many. *Bound* is a twenty-first-century articulation of that same battle, and the *Earth Walker's Handbook* is its survival guide, a map through the perilous traps set for us by sentient evil. It identifies the heresies of materialism and relativism, which have seeped into the mortar of communities of faith, gnawing away at their witness to a watching world.

Charlie's West Point training and Army service combine with his authentic spirituality and lay-theologian knowledge to whisk us into a convincing world of Guardian Angels preparing for the rigorous training they must endure to enter the human fray. As we travel with them we begin to see ourselves and our Christian culture through a different lens. We see the "forest" because in the Earth Walkers' world there are no trees to blind us to the subtlety of evil, unkindness, and compromise. There is also an invisible but clearly implied love that God, a.k.a. "The Founder," has for his creation.

Charlie plays with our sense of space and time, so don both your philosophical and theological hats as he sets the stage for the Earth Walker's entry into the world of "wo|man." He also plays with familiar names, creating a place where we can see the heroes of our faith in a different light. Read on and you will enjoy traveling with the Earth

Walkers through Boot Camp and protecting "the beautifully flawed saints" on Earth, and, at the same time, you will undoubtedly feel compelled to reflect on your own faith.

Julia Overton, Arlington, Virginia
Master of Religious Studies,
Trinity Evangelical Divinity School
Master of Education,
Harvard Graduate School of Education

Preface

I will not reveal how this rarest of documents briefly came into my possession. I can only attest that what you are beholding is an authentic reproduction of the original (save that I have added source footnotes and Bible chapter and verse(s) where applicable).

Furthermore, I must warn you that this material is not for the complacent "believer." If you are satisfied with your faith, content with your church, and confident in your eternal disposition, I strongly recommend you set this handbook down and read no further.

If, on the other hand, you question religion as you understand it, hunger for deeper fellowship, and dare examine your own salvation, read on.

Charles S. Stone
Zolden Hold, New Canaan
March 3, 2013

Abbreviations

AA	Archangel
A.K.A.	Also Known As
AM	Angelic Messenger
AAR	After Action Report
AH	Age of Harvest
AT	Age of Theophany
AOR	Area of Responsibility
AOL	Army of the Lord
APESREP	Active Lies, Propagation, Enemy Order of Battle, and Surroundings Report
BOO!	Black Ops Operatives
CO	Corporeal Operative
COTC	Corporeal Operative Training Course
DON	Descendant of Noah
D-F&D	Department of Fate & Destiny
ExTBA	Expiration to be announced
FESD	Fictional-Existence Stress Disorder
FO	Forward Observer
FSS	First Sworn Subjects
GG	Greater Gothika
Grp	Group
GS	Guardian Services
GSB	Guardian Services Brigade
GSG	Guardian Services Group

Gwhop	God who preserves
JPA	Jyeshuan Political Activist
MHS3	Ministry of Human Sociological and Spiritual Studies
PC1	Preservation Category 1
R&S	Reconnaissance & Surveillance
SCM	Spatial, Chronological, and Modulatory
SITREP	Situation Report
SPAM	Spiritual Assessment Matrix
STEP	Superreal Tactical Entry Point
TM	Team
TV	Television
UL	Unholy Legion
UTL	Untransformed Life
WMD	Weapon of Mass Destruction
WO	Winged Operative
X2	factor of two
YOW	Year of Wo|Man

Section 1

Introduction

1.1 (original) Preface

717.333(123) AH

From the Earth Walkers who precede you, welcome to Boot Camp. Despite what the Drill Seraphs may tell you, all of us want you to succeed and join the Long Earthen Line at the end of your training. Toward that end, we proffer you this compilation of advice and information to help you prepare during Orientation Phase for the storm awaiting you in Red Phase (see Appendix 7: COTC Phases).

One of only twelve physical publications produced within the Infinite Dominion, you will find reading this handbook entirely unpleasant. Its tactile nature (yes, even the so-called digital versions) will distract you, its randomness will exasperate you, and its paucity of information will frustrate you—all great preparation for operating in Finite Realm 666.

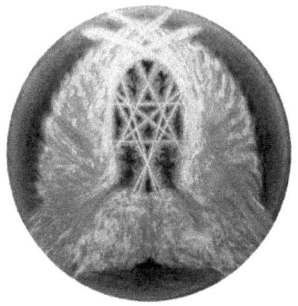

Read and memorize *Bound* during Orientation Phase; as of Red Phase your training cadre will demand that you recite any and all of its contents verbatim. Moreover, hold on to this gift to remind you that we eagerly await the day you earn the right to wear the bound-wings crest (for symbology information see our homepage: www.557GSG.org). No matter how difficult the path ahead becomes, we enjoin you to persevere. The Insurrection presses on and we need you in the fight.

The Long Earthen Line
Infinite Dominion

1.2 From the Commander

722.777(111) AH

Dear Recruit,

Congratulations on your selection for the Corporeal Operative Training Course (COTC), a.k.a. Earth Walker Boot Camp, in preparation to join the 5/57 Guardian Services Group (GSG). You have served the Heavenly Host with distinction, passed the stringent GS screening tests, and met the demanding COTC prerequisites. Should you successfully complete your training, you will join the vaunted 5/57 GSG—the only extended corporeal deployment unit in the 7th Holy Legion.

Among Guardians, Earth Walkers serve in the most demanding and dangerous role: covert, corporeal operations. Only the most capable of angels are selected to become Corporeal Operatives (COs) and COTC is the final stage of the selection process. COTC will discipline you, challenge you, and whelm you.

If you are anxious, take comfort in the fact that I felt the same way when I went through Boot Camp. Merely understanding (let alone protecting) wo|mankind required all the abilities God gave me and it took me forever, pun intended, to acclimate to Finite Realm 666. I made it; so will you.

I look forward to meeting you on Initiation Day in Gideon Hall, as do your cadre of Drill Seraphs. By the grace of God the Founder, I also look forward to pinning the bound-wings of the Earth Walker crest upon your breastplate at COTC graduation.

First in, last out!
First Captain Remiel
Commander
5th GSG, 57th GSB

1.3 Delta Team Situation Report (SITREP)

723.666(066) AH

7th Holy Legion Intell & Recon reports the Insurrection of the First is devouring mortal souls on Planet 3/Galaxy 12/Realm 666 at an alarming rate. Potent forms of spiritual counterfeit combined with personal rebellions are rapidly consuming the Descendants of Noah (DON). With diminishing prayer cover, holy combat forces struggle against an emboldened enemy. Guardian ranks stretch thin to cover the expanding wreckage of distressed souls. Accordingly, Archangel (AA) Michael secured approval from the Lord of Hosts to surge 7th Legion strength with volunteers from all corners of the Infinite Dominion.

The situation is especially dire in the materially wealthy Thrones: Greater Gothika, Isolands, and New Canaan. New Canaan, to which you will be assigned upon graduation, is the locus of power for Reversionist Jyeshuans. It is also the main effort of the Insurrection. Many of our charges there still illuminate the Pathways. However, their light steadily dims under the darkening cloud of the fallen First Archlumen. Noah's posterity needs you in this fight. Study hard. Train harder. Our foes never rest. Our charges seldom awaken.

First in, Last out!
Major Xhaliel
Team Leader
Delta Team, 5/57 GS

Section 2

Charging Charges

*Encourage, motivate,
and develop your mortal charges!*

2.1 Reflections of the Heart

THE PERSON DON KNOWS the least about is herself. She will likely possess extraordinary knowledge of the character flaws of family members, friends, rivals, acquaintances, politicians, entertainers, coworkers, supervisors, and the like, yet remain blissfully ignorant of her own. Such ignorance is an effective tool the Insurrection of the First uses to keep DON unaware of her dire condition and thusly unmotivated to seek her Maker & Redeemer. Wherefore, a critical CO mission task is to lead a charge to examine her heart.

> As water reflects the face, so one's life reflects the heart. (Prov 27:19)
> Hebraic Oral Tradition

Only by looking inward can DON know herself: flaws and foibles, values and virtues. Such self-searching takes tremendous tenacity and requires rigorous rectitude; oft demanding years of preparation before a charge is ready for this type of intrepid introspection. The investment of patience and persistence by both charge and CO is well worth the cost. When DON earnestly looks inside immediately she makes straight the way through the wilderness of her heart.

Be cautioned, however, your charge will uncover ugly truths about herself for "out of a person's heart, that evil thoughts come—sexual immorality, theft, murder, adultery, greed, malice, deceit, lewdness, envy, slander, arrogance and folly" (Mark 7:20-22). This is why the Ministry of Human Sociological and Spiritual Studies (MHS3) advises not to rush reflection for a charge who may not be ready.

To prepare her, start by finding friends who will support her. Introduce her to beautifully flawed saints and to the truth that all fall short of God's glory. Lead her to wade in the shallow waters, and when she is ready she will dive into the deep of her soul.

Once DON looks inward, generally there will be anger and anguish, but if you have prepared your charge she shall quickly transition through acceptance and then enter into a state of genuine repentance. Note, you will be able distinguish between disingenuous and ingenuous repentance by DON's actions. If she wails, cries, and throws up passionate prayers, do not expect to see a change in her behavior. If, on the other wing, she writes down her flaws and foibles onto pieces of paper and ceremonially burns them, you may very well witness the metamorphosis of peccancy to piety.

2.2 Fearless Introspection

As described in the preceding chapter, confession in the sense God the Founder intends is fearless introspection resulting in candid ownership of mistakes, flaws, and consequences, as well as acknowledgment of personal growth, blessings, and Grace. Courtesy of CO Cherub Corporal Kglmy, 2nd Section Leader, 1st Squad, Delta Team, 5/57 GSG, the excerpt below from the journal of a charge in his care provides an exemplary model of introspection wherein the author courageously and candidly seeks an authentic relationship with his Maker & Redeemer.

> Since the day I walked into Sunday service in my neighbor's living room my life has improved in ways I never thought possible. I have experienced relief from my sins such as hatred of self, jealousy, and even lust (well, some of the time that is). I have handed over character flaws like shame and received character traits like wisdom.
>
> I have come to know my Father Above in wonderfully unexpected ways. I have also confronted my biological father about his abuses and I forgave him, and ultimately built a new and wonderful relationship with him.
>
> I have seen my old religious beliefs torn to pieces and put back together in a novel but still familiar form. I have fallen in love with my wife and watched her fall out of love with me and I am now watching her come back.
>
> She is returning because by the grace of God I no longer spend every minute obsessing over my neighbor's wife—my neighbor's teenage daughter if I'm going to be honest. In fact, I often spend entire days with little to no impure thoughts or desires and I have filled the emptied space with my marriage, friendships, employment, and even happiness.
>
> There have been plenty of downturns, which happen to coincide with forgetting a lesson learned, lying to myself, isolating, rationalizing, fearing, self-pitying, resenting, and/or

fretting. I can see in those times how I edged out God, family, and friends, and how I tumbled into despair, unbelief, isolation, and bitterness. Without my daily fellowship connections I become vulnerable in my isolation and I forget that I can trust in God.

It is mind blowing how quickly I can forget hard-won lessons about God's faithfulness. I can forget that he loves me. I can forget that he moves in my life in ways no one else could. I can forget how much I love him. I can forget how it feels to make a real connection with others. I can forget how I love his creation. I can forget to seek him first and let him run my life. I can forget I am a hopeless sinner without him.

But for the most part the direction of my life since meeting Christ Jesus has been upward, away from self and toward others, away from shame and toward confidence, away from anger and toward peace, away from craziness and toward sanity, away from deception and toward honesty, away from rebellion and toward obedience, and away from hate and toward love.

2.3 Life and life

Due to the ordinate powers of existential demands (what Abraham Maslow, theorist and professor, New Canaan, 685.209 to 707.855 AH, referred to as the "hierarchy of needs" (which he almost got right)) endued by finite existence upon DON, she tends to attend to finite concerns before eternal ones. Walking in her sandals, Earth Walkers certainly empathize why this is so but we also know this inversion of priorities risks her Life for the sake of her life.

Charging Charges

> You have to decide what your highest priorities are and have the courage—pleasantly, smilingly, nonapologetically, to say "no" to other things.[1]
> Stephen Covey, author and educator,
> New Canaan, 693.975 to 723.195 AH

By the Grace of God, however, DON does not need to sacrifice forever for now, for God ordained when DON focuses on forever, he provides for now:

- "So if you faithfully obey the commands I am giving you today—to love the LORD your God and to serve him with all your heart and with all your soul—then I will send rain on your land in its season, both autumn and spring rains, so that you may gather in your grain, new wine and oil." (Deut 1:13–14)

- "Hezekiah trusted in the LORD, the God of Israel. There was no one like him among all the kings of Judah, either before him or after him. He held fast to the LORD and did not cease to follow him; he kept the commands the LORD had given Moses. And the LORD was with him; he was successful in whatever he undertook." (2 Kgs 18:5–7)

- "And why do you worry about clothes? See how the lilies of the field grow. They do not labor or spin. Yet I tell you that not even Solomon in all his splendor was dressed like one of these. If that is how God clothes the grass of the field, which is here today and tomorrow is thrown into the fire, will he not much more clothe you, O you of little faith? So do not worry, saying, 'What shall we eat?' or 'What shall we drink?' or 'What shall we wear?' For the pagans run after all these things, and your heavenly Father knows that you

---

1. Stephen Covey, *Seven Habits*, 78.

need them. But seek first his kingdom and his righteousness, and all these things will be given to you as well." (Matt 6:28–33)

Paradoxically, although many of our charges believe their Bible is the word of God, they seldom believe what their Bible tells them. With a little angelic encouragement, though, they can muster the courage to test the promises of God and we can attest the Founder always keeps his promises. It is with the joy of a parent that a Guardian watches a charge step out in faith seeking her Maker & Redeemer at the apparent sacrifice of her own needs only to discover those needs are more than met.

2.4 Prayer

Unlike us, DON can pray individually and, like us, DON can pray corporately. Individual prayer, whether internally or externally focused, is most effective at bringing about positive change within the supplicant (e.g., deeper empathy, humility, honesty, and so on). On rarer occasions, individual prayer may result in external outcome change, but that is predominantly the agency of corporate prayer.

However, when DON petitions for selfish gain (too often the case), individual prayer is predictably impotent. The same holds true for prayers that petition ill-advised results and for prayers to harm others (do not try to discover how or why DON would pray so, for no suitable answer exists).

To elucidate the distinction between prayers that avail little versus prayers that avail much, we have provided a small sampling of representative prayers from actual charges in New Canaan, 72'~AH

Prayers that Avail Little

God, please let the Raiders win. If they do win, I will go to church every Sunday for the rest of football season, thy will be done, and may Thy will be for Oakland, please, amen.

Dear God, if You can just get KO back up to $70 a share, I swear I will sell all of it, give the church 10 percent of any profit, and I will never invest in the stock market again.

Lord, what a hopeless wretch I am. My new DSL-line is a curse. I confess stayed up last night until the wee hours of this morning playing poker. I think I just needed to lose one more bundle of money to finally learn my lesson. I'm not going to tell anyone other than You, Lord but if I do go back to online gambling again (after this time, that is), I will go to twelve-step, I promise, but please don't let that happen. In fact, if you could help me make it back on Lotto I would appreciate it—I'm not asking for more than I lost (although that would be okay), I'm just asking for what I lost or even less if You think that would be a good punishment but please don't let me lose it all because then you'll force me to borrow from a less than reputable source which would probably mean I would have to gamble to have a hope at paying the interest.

Almighty God, if You will please get me out of this speeding ticket I promise I won't speed any more—at least not on purpose—unless I'm late for work.

Father God, please, Holy One, please don't let my husband check our bank account and, Father God, I promise I will never buy couture again, praise You, and that I will give to the poor, bless them, and I will proclaim your greatness,

Bound, an Earth Walker's Handbook

Almighty God, and your loving compassion, Abba Father, Thy will be done, and I also ask for forgiveness for all my sins and I confess I'm a sinner, and I repent from my sins, Merciful God, and in your holy name, Christ Jesus, I pray, amen—and I'm sorry.

Please impeach Slick Willy. He cheated on his wife while in office and deserves to suffer.

Please let Newt win the nomination. He cheated on his wives while in office but deserves a break.

Dear Lord, I don't want to give in to temptation again, so please help my wife see her duty to have sex with me whenever I want. Also, if it's not a sin, can you help her want to do more fun sexual stuff than just normal sex? (If not, I will have no choice but to find sexual outlets elsewhere).

Lord, don't let the homos take over. Please save our country from these unrepentant perverts.

God, why, why, why did it have to be the New England Patriots, again?!? You make it hard to trust You when I see such injustice in the world!

Prayers that Avail Much

Lord, I give this day to You.
Establish the work of my hands,
the steps of my feet,
the words of my mouth,
the direction of my gaze,
the thoughts of my mind,
and the affections of my heart.

I lift up the Ryan's baby girl, Kenita, who just got diagnosed with sickle cell. Please give the doctors wisdom, the family patience, and

Charging Charges

> Kenita relief. I commit to helping and ask You to show me how I can be of most use.
>
> I don't have clarity on my next steps but I do believe the answers will come out of this period of fasting, that my request will not come back unanswered. For today I know it will be enough to surrender my lust. To continue to share my secrets with trusted friends. To love my wife and my children. To rise, to eat, and to work.
>
> Heavenly Father, please bring peace to those who suffer from violence, water to those who thirst, care to the neglected children, safety to the battered wife.
>
> I pray for the people of Japan suffering in the wake of the tsunami. Please shelter, feed, and clothe those who have lost all and use the meager donations I made to maximum good.
>
> Lord, I don't want to be wrong about your will for me and I know you are not a God of confusion. Please reveal to me clearly what your will is for me today, and I will obey.
>
> Lord, I trust you to take care of me. I seek you and do your will. I know things will work out.

One of the most powerful combat multipliers available to us is mortal corporate prayer. Individual prayer is undeniably helpful and not to be dismissed in the least, but when arrayed against the sinister forces of the 6th Unholy Legion (see Appendix 6: Order of Battle, 6th Unholy Legion) we need the superior firepower afforded by the corporate prayers of wo|men.

The good news is our Jyeshuan charges often recognize this and they usually respond well to prompting to gather in prayer. For sure there will be difficulties in the execution such as lack of focus, selfish interests, and the enemy Black Ops Operatives (*BOO!)* attempts to undermine the common goal of the body of the Logos. Fortunately, Guardian Service counterinsurgency efforts, especially those of Earth Walker COs, can mitigate or even neutralize such negative forces. The tactics and methods to do so will be part of your study and practice during Orange Phase; what we want you to take away from the discussion herein is that the potential of mortal corporate prayer is outcome change.

> Then many will give thanks on our behalf for the gracious favor granted us in answer to the prayers of many. (2 Cor 1:11)
> Apostle Saul-Paul

You know the power inherent in infinite collective prayer (the four and the twenty-four, for example) but recall the revelation of these same with harps and golden bowls containing the prayers of the mortal saints! Recall King Solomon gathering the entire nation of Israel in prayer to dedicate the new halidom. Recall Martin L. King gathering the orphans of Lesser Sheba, the widows of Greater Ghana, and the pale immigrants in New Canaan to break down the barriers of pigment-based hate. Recall where two or three wo|men are gathered together in Jyeshua, he is there among them!

Delta Team, responsible for the New Canaan AOR, thus endeavors to encourage corporate prayer among our charges at all times and under all circumstances. There is, perhaps, no single greater contribution we can make toward successful mission execution (see Appendix 3: Mission Statement, Delta Team, 5/57 GSG).

2.5 Communion

Finite creation as manifest in Realm 666 is a dynamic, interdependent, closed system* relying on coordinated interaction

Charging Charges

to sustain itself. As such, all elements are fundamentally related, connected, and integrated within the whole.

> All things are interwoven with each other; a sacred bond unites them; there is scarcely one thing that is isolated from another. Everything is coordinated, everything works together in giving form to the one universe. The world order is a unity made up of multiplicity: God is one, pervading all things; all being is one, all law is one . . . and all truth is one.[2]
> Marcus Aurelius, ruler and philosopher,
> Palatine (GG), 32.507 to 54.057 AH

By design, the sentient steward of Realm 666, wo|man, is a social creature. In fact, physically, emotionally, mentally, and spiritually speaking, wo|man needs interpersonal communion in the same way she needs organic nourishment. In her unborn state, however, a wo|man is an isolated organism, and thus is severely impaired when interpreting and navigating the environments about her if she cannot, or will not, socialize with others. Our charges uniformly understand this regarding their own offspring, and thus employ social fellowships such as the family, schools, teams, and clubs to teach, prepare, and equip them to function as adults.

On the other wing, they are less uniform in their ken and approach toward their own social needs, especially spiritual ones. For example, as children they may receive religious instruction and participate in fellowship but, as they "mature" into adults, many come to believe they are better off working out their relationship alone with God the Founder.

Such unfortunates fail to recognize their carnal bodies are constructed to represent the spiritual union of all God's mortal children as manifest in the body of the Logos. To an individual organ or a disintegrated body, experiences

2. Aurelius, *Meditations*, 77.

or events are meaningless; only an integrated body can interpret and give meaning to existential experiences. For example, ears hear crackling, hands feel warmth, nostrils smell smoke, eyes see dancing light, the mind analyzes and labels the source "fire," experience interprets context, and wisdom determines the appropriate response: break out the fire extinguisher or the marshmallows.**

Similarly, without interpersonal communion within the body of the Logos, spiritual reality (or Reality) eludes the individual wo|man. Corporately, however, wo|men can holistically experience and interpret spiritual realities about them, thereby giving these experiences meaning. Such meaning transcends Illusory Reality—wo|man's existential experience—briefly elevating her into the Reality (see 6.1: Order of Realities). In Reality, therefore, wo|man only exists in interactions or, as AA Raphael likes to say: "Apart from communion, DON is naught."

> . . . the individual is defined only by his relationship to the world and to other individuals; he exists only by transcending himself, and his freedom can be achieved only through the freedom of others. He justifies his existence by a movement which, like freedom, springs from his heart but which leads outside of him.[3]
> Simone de Beauvoir, author,
> Greater Gothika, 685.209 to 713.699 AH

Consequently, for our earthly charges to touch Infinity, they must interact, a.k.a. commune, with one another.*** Social units, such as friendships, family, corporate labor, social groups, competitive teams, and marriage, are tremendously useful tools to ignite DON's innate desire for holy communion. Ideally, you can then move your charge

---

3. Beauvoir, *Ethics*, 156.

Charging Charges

toward spiritual fellowship in which she can experience communal Reality.

> And let us consider how we may spur one another on toward love and good deeds, not giving up meeting together, as some are in the habit of doing, but encouraging one another – and all the more as you see the Day approaching. (Heb 10:24–26)
> Hebraic Oral Tradition

Beware, however, for the Insurrection's *BOO!* circulate counterfeit connections, including false religions, criminal gangs, and extramarital affairs to misdirect DON toward self-destructive behaviors (sexually based counterfeit is highly intoxicating for it offers the illusion of union).

Regardless of the basis of the counterfeit, without interdiction DON will slip back into (or remain in) Illusory Reality. The paradox is the more DON seeks to connect via spiritual counterfeit, the more isolated she becomes. When the isolation becomes severe, we must move quickly as DON will be in jeopardy of self-terminating her corporeal existence (no, that is not a typographical error—see prequisite media *The Noonday Demon* and *The Bell Jar* for insight into this bizarre human behavior). This is the point at which to arrange a coincident meeting of an old friend, a call from a close family member, or the touch of a kind stranger or strangel. The smallest interaction in this state can spark DON's desire for communion with others and with God, and, thereby, preserve her life and, quite possibly, her Life.****

* Closed since the last aeon's planar collision with Realm 667.

** Gooey treats similar to *manna-honey-milk-bombs.*

*** Communion with creation (meditation) and communion with Real-beings (including prayer) will also do the trick, but generally not to the exclusion of interpersonal communion.

**** For a list of key warning signs that a wo|man's life or Life may be in danger, see Appendix 8: Charge Alarm Signals.

2.6 Love, Blatantly Divine

As stated in the preceding chapter, DON needs to connect with others and with her Maker & Redeemer in order to breach Finite Realm 666 into Infinity and, ultimately, in order to find her way to her Eternal Home. The purest mortal form of communion is love.

Mortal base love is simply positive affect.* It is commonly observed between friends but may be found in any relationship. As it is highly dependent on reciprocation, it is seldom unidirectional. Base love is not generally considered to be communion.

Committed love, however, is a form of communion. Whereas base love merely requires acceptance of innate and involuntary positive affect, committed love requires personal volition; in other words, committed love is a choice. This choice leads to action in the form of giving—giving of oneself for the betterment of others. Committed love is commonly observed between spouses, family members, and close friends and it may be uni- or bidirectional. Such love survives the challenges of human frailty, enduring and forgiving injury. Committed love fuels the flame of Life within the soul, giving purpose, joy, and meaning to mortal existence.

> To find meaning in life, you have to be actively giving members of your communities. Neither your life nor the world you live in just happens. You control the quality of your lives and your communities. It is only in giving to others that

Charging Charges

you can find meaning and satisfaction in what
you do.[4]

> Sonia Sotomayor, justice,
> New Canaan, 701.011 to ExTBA AH

As committed love matures either between two persons (bidirectional) or from one to another (unidirectional), it takes on coupled consciousness in the case of the former and subject-object convergence in the case of both. Such prodigal love tears down the fiction of individuality whereupon mortals flirt with Holy Union and become, if only intermittently, one as we are one. Prodigal love inspires parents to sacrifice personal dreams for those of their children, spouses to stand by one another through severe trials, and soldiers to offer their lives for others.

> Greater love has no one than this: to lay down
> one's life for one's friends. (John 15:13)
>
> Jyeshua

At its zenith, prodigal love shatters the walls of tri-dimensional (space-time-energy) creation, whisking the mortal soul to Reality and connecting life to Life. Flooded with love, DON can connect with those who are spatially separated from her. Mothers, for example, can connect with a child millions of cubits away, sensing when she might be ill, imperiled, or exuberant. DON can even love (and be loved by) those beyond the veil of life. Few wo|men, however, recognize the power of love over death. An exemplary and eloquent exception is Rossiter Worthington Raymond, politician and hymn writer, New Canaan, 660.372 to 688.862 AH

> There is trial and burden and struggle and pain
> For us on this earthly shore;

---

4. Sotomayor, "NYU Commencement," para. 9.

> But we surely some day shall meet again
> The dear ones gone before;
> And even in the midst of the heavenly throng
> Our own we shall find and know;
> For love is steadfast, and love is strong,
> And love will never let go!
> 						Rossiter Worthington Raymond

Love, the Founder's blatant signature, is the soul's sole possession to survive death. Love unifies and elevates mortals to the Holy, and therefore gives meaning, Life, and hope to the Descendants of Noah.

* DON considers mutual attraction to be the base form of love, but that is merely a biochemical, venereal urge common to nearly all superreal organic species—in the words of Tina Turner, bard, New Canaan, 696.532 to ExTBA AH, "What's love got to do with it?"[5]

2.7 Spiritual Development

Just as a physical infant is only aware of what is directly in front of her, a spiritual infant is similarly myopic. Thence, we promote DON's spiritual maturation by placing and keeping the words of God in front of her. Key passages from extent scriptures will coax an infantile charge from spiritual gestation through progressively higher phases of development (see Appendix 10: AA Raphael's Spiritual Assessment Matrix [SPAM]). As a COTC graduate you will be well versed in the vast array of armaments that extent scriptures provide; for now we invite you to study and consider some of the most efficacious ones:

- Blessed is the one who does not walk in step with the

---

5. Title of song written by Terry Britten and Graham Lyle, licensed by Alfred Publishing and Hal Leonard Corporation.

Charging Charges

wicked or stand in the way that sinners take or sit in the company of mockers, but whose delight is in the law of the Lord, and who meditates on his law day and night. That person is like a tree planted by streams of water, which yields its fruit in season and whose leaf does not wither. Whatever they do prospers. (Ps 1:1–3)

- Therefore confess your sins to each other and pray for each other so that you may be healed. The prayer of a righteous person is powerful and effective. (Jas 5:16)

- "Love the Lord your God with all your heart and with all your soul and with all your mind." This is the first and greatest commandment. And the second is like it: "Love your neighbor as yourself." All the Law and the Prophets hang on these two commandments. (Matt 22:37–40)

- Let your eyes look straight ahead; fix your gaze directly before you. Give careful thought to the paths for your feet and be steadfast in all your ways. Do not turn to the right or the left; keep your foot from evil. (Prov 4:25–27)

- Everyone comes naked from their mother's womb, and as everyone comes, so they depart. They take nothing from their toil that they can carry in their hands. (Eccl 5:15)

- But whatever was to my profit I now consider loss for the sake of Christ. (Phil 3:7)

- For God so loved the world that he gave his one and only Son, that whoever believes in him shall not perish but have eternal life. (John 3:16)

Section 3

Stumbling Blocks
Learn what DON commonly trips over.

3.1 Boxing God

God is the Eternal I Am, Author of All, Engineer of the Infinite Dominion and the finite realms, Source of All Consciousness, Sire of Wo|man, Ruler, King, Judge, Almighty . . . and, for a flap of a wing, human. Surprisingly, this last title dominates DON's conception of God the Founder. In fact, as documented by MHS3, DON's view of God is highly anthropomorphic and informal.

While personification of—and familiarity with—Divinity is healthy in appropriate measure, in disproportionate measure it obfuscates the relative position of a pismire to the Lord of Hosts and, due to its inherent informality, hinders genuine relationship development between wo|man and God wherein fear, awe, and respect are the order of the day. C. S. Lewis, author and layman, Hreyisles (GG), 681.557 to 705.298 AH, understood informality to be a tool

Stumbling Blocks

of the Adversary as expressed in many of his works, including the not so fanciful *Screwtape Letters*.

> They [men] can be persuaded that the bodily position makes no difference to their prayers.[1]
> Screwtape

Another popular perception of the Founder, in this case Earth-wide, is that of Judge, which is an accurate title but DON's perception of this term is severely skewed. DON personifies "Judge," rendering a veritably blasphemous perspective of a fault-finding, petty, and overbearing divine umpire. When combined with the informal viewpoint in New Canaan, the umpire morphs into a brow-furrowing, finger-wagging, foot-stomping, frowning father figure. This misconception fuels self-loathing and a counterproductive fear of God, pushing DON away from, rather than toward, her Maker & Redeemer. In addition, it leads DON to attribute consequences of her own actions to divine cameral punishment, yielding another faulty perspective of God: Punisher.

You see, DON holds to the childish notion that all her infractions (real or imagined) result in reprobation, failing to recognize the significantly larger role her decisions and actions, and those of others, play in generating negative consequences (and positive for that matter). Likewise, she ignores the stark reality that the primary outcomes of the Fall of the Stars & Wo|man under the revolting First Archlumen is death, entropy, and suffering, and these three form the fundamental basis of mortal life on Earth: tragedy.

Instead of recognizing the stark realities of fallen life, DON erroneously chooses to ascribe life's turbulence and calamities to heavenly punishment (or the "Devil's" misdoings). This makes it very difficult for DON to develop spiritually because rather than own a mistake and learn from

---

1. Lewis, *Screwtape*, 29.

the consequences of her action, she considers the matter resolved: the "sin" is punished, the scales are balanced, and so forget and repeat.

By the flight, an interesting albeit delusional derivation of the "Punisher" perspective is the belief that God punishes one's fellows for the failings of oneself. For example, DON might operate a mechanized chariot under the influence of fermented barley and while impaired accidentally cause damage to another's property. That same evening her favorite professional baseball* team loses a game to arch rivals; DON will then blame herself, attributing the loss as divine punishment for her personal, moral transgression. Curiously, this type of self-aggrandized and imagined commination has a salubrious side effect: DON will not "drink and drive" fore her team's next game.

Another common false conception of God is political activist. Reversionist Jyeshuans in New Canaan disregard that extent scriptures reveal the Logos led an apolitical life, focusing on the Kingdom of God and not the Empire of Rome. The extent of his involvement in local governance was "give back to Caesar what is Caesar's" (Matt 22:21). Jyeshuans in contemporary New Canaan, however, bombard God the Founder with far more prayer requests for intervention in their political systems than for intervention in their lives (see 3.7: The Wrong Government). They believe God has staunch interests in their politics, and, as incredulous as it may sound, they believe the King of Kings desires them to spread (by force if necessary) a pagan form of government, democratic popularism, to other nations.

Finally we come to one of the saddest misconceptions of God—that of humorless bore. Jyeshuans, and nearly all other religions by the flight, perceive God to be solely soulfully serious, and devoid of spontaneity, fun, and humor. The Founder we know to be creative and jovial, DON views as predictable and dull (reinforced in New Canaan by the combination of long sermons and uncomfortable pews). Out of misplaced fears of blasphemy, they overlook seriocomic divine intervention: Sarah's elderly pregnancy, Balaam's talking donkey, and feeding the five thousand with five loaves and two fish.

> God has brought me laughter, and everyone who hears about this will laugh with me. (Gen 21:6)
> Sarai, mother of Isaak

The aforementioned perceptions—familiar human, shaming judge, petulant punisher, political activist, and humorless bore—plus a few more you will learn about in Academic Phase, place God, if you will, in a tidy box. Normally taken off the shelf once a week on Sunday mornings (save in times of crises), this box keeps God from behaving unpredictably, from challenging DON's tightly held beliefs, and from upsetting faith in the status quo. In reality, of course, it actually serves to blind DON to God the Founder as he chooses to manifest himself.

This is precisely the reason DON seldom recognizes divinity in the Age of Harvest, just as she did not recognize the Logos as flesh in the Age of Theophany. By his own design, God comes to wo|man in unexpected ways—in "unorthodox" ways—and she would do well to doubt what fits in her god-box and open her heart to what does not.

* Team sport played by athletically endowed but often poorly physically conditioned men.

3.2 Self-Loathing

New Canaan Jyeshuans maintain a peculiar disdain for themselves that is unparalleled outside Realm 666. According to MHS3, although Jyeshuan theology espouses the opposite, in practice it advocates, "Hate the sin, but hate the sinner even more, especially when the sinner is you." Clerics and laymen alike have mistaken humiliation for humility, confusing themselves with the rubbish Apostle Saul-Paul mentioned in reference to his pursuits—not himself—before knowing the Logos in the penultimate incarnation. As the Apostle Saul-Paul was, by his own admission, the worst of sinners, it is effrontery for a Jyeshuan to think she bests his worst, but this fact is an easy obstacle for DON's hubris to breach.

The common Jyeshuan values self-loathing because, in her perverse logic, it is authorized simony: hating herself helps balance the scales weighted unfavorably by her "sin." In fact, if she heaps enough gall of bitterness upon herself (even referring to herself—and we are not making this up—as a portion of excrement), she imagines she can earn her way to Preservation through self-abuse offered in exchange for divine pity.

> You must have a very real scorn for self, if you are to prevail against flesh and blood.[2]
> Thomas à Kempis, cleric, Greater Gothika, 492.357 to 525.595

As another powerful tool of the Insurrection of the First, self-loathing does not preserve; rather, it destroys. It results in sundry outcomes such as physical and psychological stress, immune deficiencies, anxiety, anger, violence, social alienation, spiritual separation, depression, and self-termination.

The Jyeshuan self-loathing ethos becomes even more bewildering when you consider the egregious arrogance it takes for DON to exempt herself from "for God so loved the world, that he gave his one and only son" (John 3:16) believing she alone is exceptional to God's love—she alone is not worthy of Redemption. Such a person refuses to recognize

---

2. Kempis, *Imitation of Christ*, 155.

Stumbling Blocks

that her Maker & Redeemer sacrificed his purity, throne, and life for her; she is, therefore, worthwhile! In other words, if God loves wo|man, should not wo|man love herself?

> Then God said, "Let us make mankind in our image, in our likeness, so that they may rule over the fish in the sea and the birds in the sky, over the livestock and all the wild animals, and over all the creatures that move along the ground." (Gen 1:26)
>
> Antediluvian Oral Tradition

The truth is that each man and woman is made in the image of God, and to hate oneself is to hate God. Yes, the descendants of Adam rebel but as the descendants of Noah they also seek righteousness. Thus both rebellion and righteousness are the inheritance of wo|mankind. One is the posterity of Adam and the other of Noah, and were the latter not so, DON's Maker & Redeemer would not have gone to such lengths to reclaim his children for the Infinite Dominion and for Eternity.

What is an Earth Walker to do therefore? We must take every opportunity to help a charge recognize her inherent value. Encourage DON to see the positive in and of herself. Tell her to look in the mirror and say "I love you." If she refuses, remind her she is refusing her own Creator. If she concedes that point but does not believe she can love herself, tell her to say the words anyway, or to "act as if." God will honor her courage and belief will soon follow.

3.3 Jyeshuan Perspective on Conflict

The fallen state of Realm 666 demands conflict if DON is to rise above lawlessness and rebellion; yet, most Jyeshuans govern their conduct with an underlying assumption that conflict is to be avoided—that conflict is ungodly. Rather than risk a heated disagreement, a Jyeshuan will oft feign appreciation and then dance lightly around the subject at hand, valuing the pretence of accord over the benefits of dissention. You will observe this in church governance, Bible studies, and social interaction (you will not, however, observe conflict avoidance within the Jyeshuan family unit).

It seems that modern Jyeshuans hold the notion that to challenge one another is akin to "sin." They will suffer others' infractions (imaginary or real) without public confrontation but then, in private settings, complain about the know-it-all, the center-of-the-universe, or the loudmouth. Naturally such behavior weakens their fellowship by not only fomenting derisive and destructive gossip but, moreover, by crippling the fellowship's ability to grow, mature, and make prudent decisions—all difficult to do without challenging one another.

The impact of conflict avoidance has also devastated the greater church on Earth, allowing diseased members to fester and poison the entire body of the Logos. No physician would knowingly transplant a diseased organ and, if somehow she did, she would seek to cure the disease or remove the organ entirely. In the same way, the Apostle Saul-Paul admonished the Corinthians to cast out the unrepentant man who was with his father's wife. Yet, somehow, Jyeshuans miss—dismiss—this scriptural admonition as well as other examples of "godly" conflict such as Nathan and King David, Apostles Peter and Saul-Paul, and Jyeshua and the Pharisees.

We believe Jyeshuan predilection for the appearance of congruence stems from a false impression that the Logos came to bring peace; shunning the fact God donned the flesh of wo|man to bring division. Only division, necessarily attended by strife, can separate wheat from chaff, rebellious from righteous, death from life.

Stumbling Blocks

> Do you think I came to bring peace on earth? No, I tell you, but division. From now on there will be five in one family divided against each other, three against two and two against three. They will be divided, father against son and son against father, mother against daughter and daughter against mother. (Luke 12:51–53)
>
> Jyeshua

Through division:

- The Eternal Ghost of God separated light from darkness.
- The Almighty cast the First Archlumen from Dominion.
- Abraham fathered three faiths.
- Moses freed Israel from Egypt.
- Lawless Israel was subjugated by Babylon.
- A remnant was preserved.
- Jyeshua sent out the Twelve.
- The Jyeshuan church split (therefore fit) into East and West.
- Martin Luther sparked the Reversionist division.
- Reversionists emigrated to New Canaan.

During Green Phase you will have the opportunity to practice disabusing your charges of their misconceptions regarding division and conflict. You will experiment with various methodologies to encourage them to challenge each other in the spirit of godliness and you will model appropriate conflictive interaction. The key factor to all successful confrontation is respect, for it keeps DON focused on the issues rather than the personalities. Respect listens. Respect considers. Respect honors.

From this foundation, DON can challenge without insult and pursue the greater good. When (not if!) you graduate Boot Camp, make it a priority to teach your charges to avoid the doldrums of peace-at-all-costs and navigate, instead, the storm-tossed waters of conflict with respect for others and confidence in the Pilot.

3.4 Within the Law

DON desires simplicity when it comes to moral judgments, preferring absolutes to the perceived rigors of personal decision making. Thus she defers judgment to external sources that, in her estimation, apply to her station such as the ten commandments, civil law, social mores, ethical philosophies, codes of conduct, honor codes, and the like. The fact DON often fails to abide by these governances is immaterial to our concerns; what is material is that DON routinely abdicates her responsibility for moral decision-making entirely to external authority, which can lead DON down ruinous paths.

According to MHS3 there are three primary reasons DON prefers external authority over personal decision making:

1. It appears easier than determining for oneself what to do.
2. It removes personal responsibility for negative consequences.
3. It supports DON's misguided belief that moral reality is twofold.

Many of our charges believe blind adherence to external rules to be less arduous than analyzing, assessing, and acting; though in our experience the plain truth is it is far

Stumbling Blocks

simpler to listen to the Ghost of God than to apply static and often inapposite external principles. As you are beginning to see, however, DON's ability to deny truths appears limitless; indeed, it would behoove you to abort any attempt to reckon its bounds. Rather, focus on why she denies certain truths. In this case, DON desperately seeks to avoid the cognitive labor, emotional strain, and spiritual intimacy required to make tough decisions; she prefers to pretend there is always an absolute and authoritative right answer within the law.

As a perceived added bonus, Don believes following an external rule relieves her of personal responsibility—after all, how can she be held responsible for an unfortunate (even if foreseeable) result if she was "just following orders"?

Next, let us examine the myth of twofold moral reality that pervades religious adherents worldwide. In her dormant and infantile spiritual phases (see Appendix 10: AA Raphael's Spiritual Assessment Matrix [SPAM]), DON believes ethical standards are provisioned and meted in absolutes; thereby, choices are binary: either right or wrong. Accordingly, she views scripture and other governance in fixed, literal terms and the world about her as "black & white." Interpretation, ambiguity, and gray areas are forbidden!

An evitable result of the myth of twofold moral reality is injury, for despite DON's "best intentions" to do what is right, rigid application of external governance can produce harmful effects; e.g., candor with a culinary-challenged hostess. Even those who apply solely the Bible to their decision making can err horrifically; e.g., protecting and practicing human slavery.

In defense of DON, extent scriptures do provide numerous external moral rules to govern behavior, from which it could be inferred that wo|man should adhere to such rules absolutely. However, these same scriptures also provide examples of righteous deviation from the law:

1. Rahab hid the spies of Jyoshua and lied to the soldiers of Jyericho searching for them.
2. David at Nob fed his soldiers consecrated bread from the priest.
3. David at Gath deceived the royal court and King Achish to believe he was a lunatic.
4. King Hezekiah had Israel celebrate the lost tradition of Passover despite all had not been purified; the Lord of Mercy honored Hezekiah's request to "pardon everyone who sets his heart on seeking God . . . even if he is not clean according to the rules of the sanctuary" (2 Chr 30:18–19).
5. Jyeshua healed many of their illnesses on the Sabbath.

> Was not even the prostitute Rahab considered righteous for what she did when she gave lodging to the spies and sent them off in a different direction? (Jas 2:25)
> Brother Jyames

Lastly, some external rules, despite their pervasiveness and persuasiveness, are simply lies of the Dark Labs spread by the *BOO!* Take for example the nearly universal social more of ex post facto collusion within familial and social units. This more states, more or less, that if you discover one of your relatives, friends, or acquaintances has broken a rule, you must not report said violation to any authority or take any action that might result in prosecutorial measures. This applies to even the most abhorrent behavior such as theft, assault, and murder (do not attempt to fathom this, for it is beyond angelic comprehension).

More incredibly, DON traduces those who report transgressors with libelous labels such as "rat," "tattle tale," and "fink" because reporting unethical and unlawful behavior is

Stumbling Blocks

immoral under the governance of this wildly fantastical, yet widely held social more. This vilification of the good citizen consistently achieves its villainous aim: the protection and perpetuation of lawlessness and rebellion. In fact, this perverse principle of silence serves as the foundation of all social corruption: silence is essential to sustain all organized extortion, exaction, exploitation, execration, and exclusion.

> It may well be that we will have to repent in this generation, not merely for the vitriolic works and violent actions of the bad people who bomb a church in Birmingham, Alabama, or shoot down a civil rights worker in Selma, but for the appalling silence and indifference of the good people who sit around.[3]
> Martin Luther King Jr., prophet,
> New Canaan, 692.879 to 707.124 AH

What is an Earth Walker to do? Encourage your charges to challenge malevolent societal norms. Remind your charges that the laws of God are to aid them and not to master them; that "the Sabbath was made for man, not man for the Sabbath" (Mark 2:27). Encourage them to work through the angst and anguish of moral decisions. Reassure them when they venture into the muddied gray waters of ethical dilemmas, they need only listen to the whispers of the Ghost of God, who faithfully leads the way.

3.5 Frenzied

As you are now experiencing in simulated, low-intensity finite environments during Orientation Phase, submission to finite time and tri-dimensional Superreality (see 6.1: Order of Realities) limits existence beyond anything you could have

---

3. King, *Remaining Awake*, 7.

imagined: it reduces all experience, interaction, and production to singularities. Multiplicity, if it can be called that, can only occur linearly. Given the extreme shock of linear existence, a leading cause of Red Phase washouts is finite time.*

Regrettably for Earth Walker candidates, experientially understanding time is essential to understanding Illusory Reality and, more importantly, understanding one of the greatest threats to DON's eternal disposition. This is because while entropy, on a spiritual and physical level, relentlessly tears down DON's spiritual and physical girders in parallel (see 6.6: Entropy), DON must choose among which girders to rebuild and maintain since her actions can only occur serially. Given the ordinate powers of existential demands, DON will necessarily attend to the most compelling ordination, physical health, first and the least compelling, spiritual health, last, if at all.

Now that you have experienced physical hunger you undoubtedly empathize as to why this is so, but the hazard is that DON will forgo any attention to her spiritual health. Take, for example, these e-pistle excerpts between two earnest and faithful Jyeshuans.

> -----Original Message-----
> From: Carmen.Lin [mailto:Carmen.Lin@compyouserve.com]
> Sent: Friday, July 7, 2000 12:34 PM
> To: 'Esther Thomas'
> Subject: check in
>
> Hi Esther, I've had a few hard days lately. Work has been very busy and pressured, and I've really been resenting the amount of time it takes from my personal life. I need quiet, alone time and just don't get any. Even on vacation I didn't get by myself enough. So I've been irritable at work. I think I'm calming down a bit but I have

a long way to go. I'm also finding that I'm not sleeping enough. I have real trouble getting up in the morning, so I've cut my prayer time short and found myself rushing to get out the door . . .

-----Original Message-----
From: Esther.Thomas [mailto:Esther.Thomas@GTE.com]
Sent: Friday, July 7, 2000 3:21 PM
To: 'Carmen Lin'
Subject: RE: check in

Carmen, I know what you mean. Malik has kids from all over the neighborhood running through my house each and every day. Jerome calls every Sunday threatening to quit C.I.T. because he "don't fit in." Sharise is dating a much older boy and Maurice is working two jobs to make ends meet, but they never meet! So I just started working the late shift at Parcels and now I never see Maurice. Only time I see him and only time I talk to God is for two hours on Sunday at First Temple Baptist. I wish it was different, I truly do, but life gets in the way . . .

These two women represent an increasingly frenetic pace at which DON lives her life as civilization and technologies rapidly grow on the eve of the Age of Harvest (just think if we didn't intervene at Babel!). In this case, Esther and Laura's Guardians, Staff Seraph Ameok and Seraph First Class Fhilgie, collaborated and inspired them to form a Wednesday evening Bible study, rotating at each others' homes. It grew to half a dozen regulars and half a dozen part-timers, and both women now set aside thirty minutes each day to pray alone.

To emulate this success with your charges, continually remind them that their spiritual lives require nourishment just as desperately as their physical lives, even though the pangs are much less intense. "Just a few minutes of prayer a day will keep the First away," AA Raphael likes to say—and we certainly agree.

*The leading cause of Red Phase washouts is spiritual isolation as discussed in 6.5: Principal Existential Laws, 666th Superreal Plane.

3.6 The Deaf God

One of the chief complaints you will overhear your charges level against God the Founder is that their prayers go unanswered. They will assume a number of blasphemous and implausible reasons: God is not listening, God does not care, God is punishing them, God abandoned them, God is dead, God never was. They will seldom assume, however, the actual reason: namely, they have separated themselves from their Maker & Redeemer, and thus he has excecated his eyes and deafened his ears to them.

> Your iniquities have separated
> you from your God;
> your sins have hidden his face from you,
> so that he will not hear. (Isa 59:2)
>
> Iza'ah

> Then they will cry out to the LORD,
> but he will not answer them.
> At that time he will hide his face from them
> because of the evil they have done. (Mic 3:4)
>
> Michah

Stumbling Blocks

If DON has an inkling of her spiritual separation, she will likely listen to the counsel of Elifaz, Bildahd, and Zopharr: she is being punished for her "sins." In this case, remind her that God cannot conjoin with lawlessness and rebellion, ergo the Sacrifice, the Preservation, and the Almighty's present tone-deafness to her voice. DON need merely repent in order to regain the ear of her Maker & Redeemer.

Often, though, DON mistakes lip service for repentance: she will audibly confess and apologize, and she will feel badly, but she will not turn away. Rather, she will continue to abide in rebellion; whereat the Founder will continue to mute her pleas.

> In that day I will become angry with them and forsake them; I will hide my face from them. (Deut 31:17)
>
> JYWH

At this point she may conclude the Ancient of Days has withdrawn; if this is the case, speak to her the truth she already knows but forgot (forgetfulness of truths, by the flight, is a frailty common to wo|man): God does not move, wo|man does. Usually this message resonates with DON and she may become open to other spiritually healthy activities. This is the time to talk about communion, prayer, reading, and introspection. If she listens, her actions will lead to sincere repentance and reconnection with her Maker & Redeemer who will, in turn, hear her voice once again.

> Who is a God like you,
> who pardons sin and forgives the transgression
> of the remnant of his inheritance?
> You do not stay angry forever
> but delight to show mercy.
> You will again have compassion on us;
> you will tread our sins underfoot

and hurl all our iniquities into the depths of the sea. (Mic 7:18–19)

Michah

3.7 The Wrong Government

DON commonly misdirects her energies from the Kingdom of God to the nations of wo|men. This is particularly true for the Jyeshuans of New Canaan. According to MHS3, Jyeshuan Political Activists (JPAs) disproportionately prioritize the government of wo|man over the government of God in nearly all their activities; this premise is supported by Table 2.7-1, which presents the salient findings from an MS3 study conducted in 721~ AH of Jyeshuan life currency (time) expenditure in New Canaan.

Allocation of Life Currency for a Typical JPA by Salient Activity

Activity	Spiritual Focus	Political Focus	Other
Watching TV	5%	60%	35%
"Web surfing"	10%	40%	50%
Talking w/ family	10%	40%	50%
Talking w/ friends	5%	40%	55%
Reading	20%	30%	50%
Praying	25%	50%	25%

Table 2.7-1

JPAs supply themselves with several arguments as to why their first fruits should go to the politics of wo|man, but primarily they believe that since governance significantly impacts the spiritual health of the governed, those within

Stumbling Blocks

their religious division should be heavily engaged in political activism instead of trusting God the Founder to do the job.

> Let everyone be subject to the governing authorities, for there is no authority except that which God has established. The authorities that exist have been established by God. (Rom 13:1)
> Apostle Saul-Paul

The passion of JPAs is so intense and their motives so genuine (generally) that many an Earth Walker has been persuaded to agree that devotion of significant personal energies toward human governance is merited. Some even suggest that due to the rise of pagan democratic popularism, the apolitical example Jyeshua set in the Age of Theophany no longer applies. Guard yourself now against this misconstruction, for the energy and attention men and women squander on temporal politics robs their eternal livelihoods.

To clarify, we do not mean to proscribe all political activity; indeed, a functioning government is essential for the welfare of wo|mankind. Rather, the type of behavior we dissuade is the obsessive, fanatical attention JPAs devote to their fleeting and fickle politics. Pay especial attention to those who burn with an insatiable desire to convert others to their political beliefs, to censor all dissenting beliefs, and even to dictate what others can do in the privacy of their homes—despite their rule of law advertently and staunchly protects such individual freedoms!

> If the First Amendment means anything, it means that a State has no business telling a man, sitting alone in his own house, what books he may read or what films he may watch. Our whole

> constitutional heritage rebels at the thought of giving government the power to control men's minds.[4]
>
> Thurgood Marshall, justice,
> New Canaan, 685.209 to 716.255 AH

Choosing to evangelize the causes of wo|men over the gospel of God, JPAs expend phenomenal energies persuading, enticing, pleading, egging, and pestering nearly every person encountered, and the evitable products of these browbeating behaviors include:

- Estranged personal relationships
- Homogenous social networks
- Spiritual inbreeding
- Emotional poisoning

It would seem evident that relentless and oppressive wheedling and needling serve to disaffect most acquaintances save those who are likeminded, and yet JPAs are either blind or indifferent to the alienation of so many and the similitude of the few who remain. This self-selection of uniform perspectives leads to groupthink and spiritual inbreeding wherein only socially sanctioned beliefs are allowed—diversity, conflict, contradiction, and division are not tolerated.

Spiritually steeped in insular thinking, JPAs emotionally poison themselves with a toxic brew of vitriol and vilification of those whose politics they oppose. Visit a random New Canaan watching vantage and view a campaign advertisement or visit a candidate debate, and take note of how the JPAs conduct themselves. Better yet, while on your first corporeal practicum, voice a "pro-choice" sentiment

---

4. Stanley v. Georgia, 394 U.S. 557 (1969).

Stumbling Blocks

around the church water cooler and you will be afforded the opportunity to sample these toxins first-hand.

Beyond the aforementioned hazards of Jyeshuan political activism, we should also mention that DON's personal investment in politics, especially pagan popularism, is a futile enterprise. Those of the Long Earthen Line before you can attest that wo|men are collectively incapable of selecting benevolent, spiritually healthy governors.

Beginning with the pool of those interested in competing for political position, the odds are severely weighted toward the arrogant and incompetent. The subsequent process of whittling down the pool to a short list of nominations typically elevates those who are predominantly elitist, self-impressed, and delusional. Finally, when it comes time for DON to choose among candidates, she is not only impaired to discern what lies in the heart of each candidate, she is actually predisposed to select a devil masquerading as an angel of light. She simply cannot ascertain the candidates' motives and she most likely suffers from prejudiced opinions that blind her to objective truths about the persons and issues involved. Furthermore, although she considers herself well informed, discerning, and open-minded, you will discover the typical elector is dull, dilatory, and dogmatic.

> "The first lesson you learn as a pollster is that people are stupid," said Tom Jensen of Public Policy Polling.[5]
>
> Alexander Burns, journalist,
> New Canaan, 714.064 to ExTBA AH

Given the self-destructive pitfalls of Jyeshuan Political Activism and DON's inability to nominate and elect competent representatives in pagan popularist New Canaan, we

---

5. Burns. "Voters," para. 6

strive to refocus our charges' attentions on changing their own lives rather than controlling the lives of others.

A key message we impart to DON is that her ends would be far better served by focusing energy toward knowing God the Founder, and letting him attend to the government of wo|man. This involves tremendous faith—stepping-out-of-the-boat type of faith—for she is inclined to forget and doubt that prayer, especially the prayers of many, can do more to turn over control of this fallen world to its Creator than any elector, governor, or king could ever do.

Section 4

Wo|Man: Nature & Nativity

Do your best to understand this blessed oddity among the Founder's creations.

4.1 Unborn

To borrow from Oswald Chambers, cleric and teacher, Hreyisles (GG), 672.791 to 688.496 AH, the human experience in its original unborn state can be described as "Unconscious Unreality." Physically alive while spiritually dead, these unborn souls slumber spellbound by the illusions of the fallen First Archlumen, ignorant of spiritual Reality and of their own spiritual captivity.

> MORPHEUS: The Matrix is everywhere, it's all around us, here, even in this room. You can see it out your window or on your television. You feel it when you go to work, or go to church or pay your taxes. It is the world that has been pulled over your eyes to blind you from the truth.
> NEO: What truth?

> MORPHEUS: That you are a slave, Neo. Like everyone else, you were born into bondage, kept inside a prison that you cannot smell, taste, or touch–a prison for your mind.[1]
> Wachowski Brothers, writers and filmmakers, New Canaan, 706.028/757 to ExTBA(X2) AH

The minions of the First work tirelessly to maintain their captives' dormancy through the continuous benumbing of spiritual senses to block awareness of the truth and to keep us out—no light, no warmth, no still small voice. The only media through which the Heavenly Host can reach the unborn are born Descendants of Noah, AA Gabriel's Messengers, and Earth Walker COs. All can directly converse with the unborn and reveal the underlying spiritual Reality, opening the gateway to Truth, Life, and the very Ghost of God.

4.2 Rousing and Birthing

Initial Earth Walker attempts to rouse the unborn usually fail; on the other wing, they oft succeed in fertilizing the unconscious soul with the possibility of something more—something divine. Through continued outreach by awoken wo|men, Messengers, and COs, an unborn can be sufficiently agitated to stir from her spiritual torpor. If she then searches for something divine she may reclaim, if only tacitly, her spiritual memory of the oneness of all in God's Eternal Ghost, and this is frequently a sufficient stimulus for spiritual gestation. But beware!

Immediately the enemy will attempt to abort a soul's impending birth by silencing the awoken wo|men and corporeal angels who are causing the disturbance, and you can

---

1. Wachowski and Wachowski, *Matrix*, 28.

Wo|Man: Nature & Nativity

expect unholy *BOO!* to employ blocking tactics to isolate and then lull their restless captive back into a deep sleep. Under sufficient prayer cover, however, we can penetrate enemy lines and continue to share the rousing truth and therefore foster spiritual gestation.

As an embryonic soul awakens to the truth of spiritual Reality, she becomes increasingly aware of her unity with all wo|mankind. Her experience of unity, however, is the polar opposite of what we experience, namely: unity in mutual frailty, in certain mortality, in moral infirmity, in spiritual poverty, in terrific captivity, in undeniable futility, and in ubiquitous tragedy. Hers is the fellowship of suffering which, by the inestimable love of her Maker & Redeemer, is also the fellowship of the Logos himself.

Ironically, a salient consequence of the First's Insurrection, suffering, has become a catalyst for spiritual labor, pushing a nascent soul to acknowledge her insufficiency, her bondage, and, finally, the paradoxical touchstone of spiritual birth: her own lawlessness. Lawlessness is death and yet it is the key to Life.

> For sin, seizing the opportunity afforded by the commandment, deceived me, and through the commandment put me to death. So then, the law is holy, and the commandment is holy, righteous and good. Did that which is good, then, become death to me? By no means! Nevertheless, in order that sin might be recognized as sin, it used what is good to bring about my death, so that through the commandment sin might become utterly sinful. (Rom 7:11–13)
>
> Apostle Saul-Paul

The spiritually unborn cannot connect with the righteousness of God because there are no connection points. By awakening the unborn to the Law—while it does coincidentally introduce lawlessness and therefore indictment, conviction, and condemnation—the Eternal Ghost creates the potential for gestation, birth, and Preservation because the Logos became lawlessness and, in doing so, transformed that which separates into that which connects. Through the power of God's love (which the First thought folly), God's own blasphemy (which the First thought impossible) anointed wo|man with God's own righteousness (which the First thought assailable).

Through Grace, which admittedly we angels struggle to comprehend, God the Founder transforms the unborn Descendant of Adam—the father of mortal rebellion—into newborn Descendants of Noah—the father of mortal righteousness.

The battle for DON's will, however, is far from over. Though alive, a newborn soul is not necessarily preserved for Eternity, and during her vulnerable infancy you must be prepared to fend her from the fury of the First.

4.3 Counterfeit, Rebellions, & False Practices

The Insurrection of the First sews spiritual counterfeit as cancerous seeds among spiritually infantile wo|men for the purpose of yielding bountiful human crops for demonic surfeit. Coordinated by the dreaded First Sworn Subjects (*FSS*), multiple Insurrection elements develop and deploy spiritual counterfeit. The process begins in the Dark Laboratories where Sinisterists concoct and beta-test new forms of counterfeit. When a new or revised form of counterfeit is released for general availability, the infamous *BOO!* will deploy it in the field while armored Nephilim and winged demons from the 6th Unholy Legion cover their movements (see Appendix 6: Order of Battle, 6th Unholy Legion). Prominent spiritual counterfeit circulating in New Canaan,

72'~AH, include myths and cults, drugs and alcohol, pornography, reality TV, video games, outrageous corporate bonuses, Mc-Mansions, SUVs, sycophants, slot machines, and compulsive tweeting.

As wo|men encounter such counterfeit littering their reality, they can fall prey to personal rebellions that align with their individual, innate predispositions such as idolatry, jealousy, sexual depravity, avarice, prejudice, deception, exploitation, all manner of addiction, vanity, self-worship, arrogance, hedonism, and hoarding to include that timeless favorite of DON's: tax evasion.

> Each person is tempted when they are dragged away by their own evil desire and enticed. (Jas 1:14)
>
> Brother Jyames

Personal rebellions disconnect and isolate wo|men spiritually and relationally, creating an obdurate class of souls nearly impervious to the mollifying attempts of God's Ghost. It takes direct and usually repeated confrontation from a DON or a CO to get through to a sot drunk on her personal rebellion(s). Those who refuse to listen risk spiritual death, for it is one thing to awaken spiritually but it is entirely another to accept the gift of Eternal Preservation from the Logos.

> Our part as workers for God is to open men's eyes that they may turn themselves from darkness to light; but that is not salvation, that is conversion–the effort of a roused human being. I do not think it is too sweeping to say that the majority of nominal Christians are of this order; their eyes are opened, but they have received nothing. Conversion is not regeneration.[2]

---

2. Chambers, *My Utmost*, 7.

Bound, an Earth Walker's Handbook
> Oswald Chambers, cleric and teacher,
> Hreyisles (GG), 672.791 to 688.496 AH

Those who do listen, on the other wing, will likely shed their fictional fetters forthwith as the Ghost adjures them to forsake the temporal for the Eternal. Immediately upon emancipation from personal rebellions (different than emancipation from Death), we employ techniques you will learn in Blue Phase to help novice charges spiritually develop toward maturity; whilst the Sinisterists and the *BOO!* manufacture conditions and reinforce behaviors designed to foster adoption of spiritual false practices in order to seduce spiritually awake "subjects" to slumber in Untransformed Living—a horrific static state from which it is exceedingly difficult to extract DON.

Spiritual False Practices we often encounter in New Canaan include:

- Pharisaism. Those practicing Pharisaism believe they will be preserved (a.k.a. "saved") through self-righteous condemnation of others for the same personal rebellions they practice themselves.

- Legalism. Those practicing Legalism believe they will be preserved by strictly adhering to the codified laws of their religious division.

- Cognition. Those practicing Cognition believe they will be preserved by thoroughly examining, studying, and understanding the canon of their religious division.

- Believism. Those practicing Believism believe they will be preserved by believing in their own belief.

- Homogeneity. Those practicing Homogeneity believe they will be preserved by behaving as others who espouse the same faith.

- Perfunctorism. Those practicing Perfunctorism believe they will be preserved by dutifully performing the religious rites of their particular division.

- Externalism. Those practicing Externalism believe they will be preserved by appearing pious to others.

- Genuine Insincerity. Those practicing Genuine Insincerity believe they will be preserved by genuinely wishing they were sincere in their beliefs.

As you likely have witnessed from the watching vantages, false practitioners have become harder to detect in the Age of Harvest than in the Age of Theophany. In those days one could identify a Pharisee, for example, simply by his clerical attire; whereas, presently Pharisees do not necessarily hold religious office and, by the flight, they are not necessarily sexed male. Their untransformed lives, however, reveal the reality their physical appearances and other pretences, with which you will become all too familiar, belie. In short, DON may make or have made certain statements of faith, but the manner in which she lives her life bears no appreciable difference before and after "she got saved" (as DON is apt to say). The dreadful outcome of untransformed living is that DON believes she is in communion with her Maker & Redeemer while actually remaining separated.

4.4 About Untransformed Living

Insofar as the variety of false practices described in chapter 4.3 is concerned, it merely reflects the creativity of the Sinisterists but does not, to the Earth Walker at least, obscure the common denominator of all false practices: Untransformed Living. At its root, the supporting condition of Untransformed Living is denial, and that is something we angels long to understand. Notable among DON's numerous intriguing skills is her ability to ignore a particularly uncomfortable self-truth. In the case of an Untransformed Life (UTL), it enables DON to believe she is living a spiritual life while actually living enslaved to personal rebellions. You may hear DON use the phrase "living a double life" to describe such a person, but we assure you this is a misnomer for no one can serve two masters coincidentally.

You are, undoubtedly, confused as to how DON can believe she has turned her will over to her Maker & Redeemer while her conduct clearly contradicts this premise; i.e., nothing about how she lives her life has been transformed! How could temporal, hapless, condemned, wo|man meet, follow, and serve the everlasting Holy One and yet remain unchanged and unscathed? She cannot and, therefore, a UTL does not know the Logos.

How could a UTL possibly think otherwise? Again, the flummoxing answer is denial and unfortunately we can offer little insight as to how DON actually pulls off denying blatant fact; we can only attest that she does so with shocking ease.

However, through tactics and techniques you will learn in Blue Phase, COs, in collaboration of the Ghost of God, we can shine the light, rip down the veil, and drag DON kicking and screaming out of her cave. If successful, we are perpetually ill prepared for how rankled DON can be when awoken from her dark spiritual slumber. With remarkable consistency, she self-flagellates in a misguided attempt to atone for her willful rebellion (see 3.2: Self-Loathing). Endure this tumult with DON and she will likely calm down and then, with your firm but gentle intervention, finally see her own denial.

You might hear DON call this "a moment of clarity," and that is well said for DON will clearly see her rebellion and separation from God the Founder. This is a decisive point in the battle for her soul, and we can assure you the enemy will counterattack with desperate vim and vengeance.

Employing a horrifying array of weapons, Insurrection forces will assault 7th Holy Legion combat elements directly while the *BOO!* infest DON with the Dark Lab's infamous UTL Predicates. Originally invented by the Master of Mendacity, the First himself, the UTL Predicates consist of four terrific spiritual lies that, if DON ingests, allow her to move beyond denial into a far worse UTL-supporting condition: acquiescence.

Acquiescence is deliberate rebellion without repentance. In this condition DON relies on one or more of the UTL Predicates to sustain her spiritual false practice(s) despite awareness of her own rebellion. This is a precarious position and such charges are oft lost forever when the flicker of mortal life departs their earthen vessels.

The UTL Predicates are:

1. I can't help it.
2. I'll have fun now and live rightly later.
3. I can do what I want because all my sins are forgiven (a.k.a., the Layaway Preservation Plan).
4. It's not as bad as it is.

As incredible as these statements are, DON actually believes them, or, perhaps more accurately, she wants to believe them. Although we do not subjectively understand DON's willingness to accept fantastic lies such as the UTL Predicates, we objectively comprehend that they stem from the strength of her longing to hold on to cherished personal rebellions. DON is, quite literally, willing to do anything to keep them.

If none of this makes sense to you, consider the emergence of weapons of mass destruction (WMD) in the twentieth century YOW, the most devastating of which is Internet pornography. Go to any New Canaan watching vantage, select any church of any division, and watch the droves of wo|men marching right off the cliff into the dark pit of slavery to various media containing images of nudity and sexual activity, and stories of illicit affairs and lustful intrigue. The allure and antidotes of this spiritual poison are beyond our scope herein; for now your challenge is to accept the difficult truth that certain Untransformed Lives will do absolutely anything to keep personal rebellions like pornography, and that is precisely why they so readily believe the preposterous lies of their enemy.

> Do not be so confident of atonement that you add sin to sin. Do not say, "His mercy is great and he will forgive the multitude of my sins," for both mercy and wrath are with him. (Sir 5:5–6, RSV)
>
> Ben Sira

4.5 A Vignette: WMD and UTL Predicates Combine

A useful illustration of the destructive power of the aforementioned WMD combined with the UTL Predicates can be found in this After Action Report recorded by CO Cherub Corporal Chumliel, 4th Team Leader, 3rd Squad, Delta Team, 5/57 GSG, on the *Battle for Male Reversionist Jyeshuans, Zoldan Hold*, 717~ AH.

> The 1st Celestial Group and Delta Team of the 5th Corporeal Group attacked spiritual counterfeits pornography and infidelity with the awesome firepower of a GS countermeasure called Promise Keepers, founded 715.160 AH in New Rock. The countermeasure grew rapidly, supplanting

Wo|Man: Nature & Nativity

false practices across New Canaan, from Red Thoryk to New Sodom to Bala Ledd.

On 717.716(277) we set our sights on Zoldan Hold, that whitewashed necropolis where pagan popularism is practiced, preached, and promoted, and whence it propagates across the planet. With the mighty 3/37th Squadron (the Calvary Cavalry) screening our flanks, Task Force 2/17, to which my squad was attached as corporeal scouts, initially found enormous success and routed the defending company from 1st Brigade of the 66th Armored Nephilim Division. We broke through denial of slavery to printed pornography in hundreds of thousands of men and, for a time, it seemed we would reclaim many more for the Dominion.

Then came the onslaught of the 1st Brigade counterattack, the proliferation of the UTL Predicates by the insidious *BOO!*, and the revelation of an advanced and highly lethal Dark Labs pornography delivery system know as the World Wide Web. With unprecedented speed, the Descendants of Noah turned on us.

The magnetic draw of "Internet porn" not only reclaimed former UTLs but also drew in fresh throngs of untransformed souls who eagerly grasped any and all of the UTL Predicates to keep this newfound, besotting personal rebellion. A few of them accepted that "it's not that bad," choosing to minimize the devastation pornography leveled against themselves and their loved ones. Scores more decided to "play around just a little longer and get right with the Lord later," gambling that tomorrow will become today. The vast majority either attempted to mortgage the debt already paid by their Maker & Redeemer (believing they had been granted spiritual immunity) or privately resigned themselves to

> putatively inescapable depravity (believing they had no choice but to sin).
>
> As a result, many Jyehsuans in New Canaan are still enslaved, and were it not for the gallant efforts of the Calvary Cavalry Rescue-Jumpers (see also Standing Order 5.a), I would surely be suffering the torment of demonic captivity until the Day of Judgment. These are dark times my friends. Observe your Drill Seraphs' instructions carefully and take every opportunity to prepare.
>
> Cherub Corporal Chumliel
Delta Team, 5/57th GSG

4.6 UTL and Preservation

Surprising to many an Earth Walker, not all Untransformed Lives are consumed upon mortal death. While the results we observe postmortem are not encouraging for UTLs, we are ever astonished by the souls who do show up in Abraham's Bosom. Indeed, the incalculable love of the Creator never ceases to surprise us, but the sad fact and point of discussion herein is that, by and large, UTLs suffer eternal death.

Let us also remind you that Preservation is the business of the Founder, Ghost & Logos, and we cannot know for sure if a charge is preserved ante mortem (see Appendix 9: Calculating the Probability of Preservation). On the other wing, we do know for sure a few things Preservation is not. Preservation is not lip service, Preservation is not sometime later, Preservation is not Unrepentant Living, and Preservation is not head knowledge (despite the pervasiveness of this theology throughout the Age of Harvest).

> Now, to believe is immediately an act of the intellect, because the object of that act is "the true,"

Wo|Man: Nature & Nativity

which pertains properly to the intellect. Consequently faith, which is the proper principle of that act, must reside in the intellect.[3]

Thomas Aquinas, cleric and philosopher,
Palatine (GG), 435.743 to 453.641 AH

Wherefore does an UTL not live in fear and trembling before God the Founder? Unfortunately, whereas you may have grave concern over the state of Preservation for a charge, she is most likely living in preservation jeopardy—a spiritual condition overshadowed by Abaddon, supported by false practices, and marked by complacency (or misplaced confidence) about where she is bound after her mortal expiration.

Many such unfortunates practice lip service Preservation, or, as the Drill Seraphs would most certainly prefer to hear from a recruit, Perfunctorism. They repeatedly make statements of faith and occasionally perform rites such as a dousing of water, and yet go about their merry ways unchanged (at least from what we can observe), thinking all will be different once they expire just because they went through the motions as prescribed.

Others sustain their state of preservation jeopardy through faith in homogenous fellowship, drawing assurance of Preservation from their self-created social surroundings; specifically, wo|men of the same faith who, particularly in church, act congruently, speak of one accord, and, most unnerving to the unprepared Earth Walker, dress alike. These poor homos, as we lovingly refer to them, take great comfort that they "are going to heaven" since they are like their self-selected comparison-others who are also confident they are "going to heaven" since they are like their self-selected comparison-others who are. . . . Tautology notwithstanding, the fact that a homo's behavior outside of

3. Aquinas, *Summa Theologica*, 40.

church contradicts her behavior inside church escapes her own attention (again, there are some things we simply cannot understand and we find it best in such circumstances to simply acknowledge wo|man is truly a bemusing creation).

Perhaps the most common false practice used to support preservation jeopardy is Believism: the belief that "I will be saved by believing that I believe in Jesus." Earth Walker recruits generally have a hard time believing DON actually believes this nonsensical belief; regrettably, we believe she does. Through declarations and demonstrations, DON will reinforce her belief in her belief in the Logos, all the while never actually believing in him or believing him as evidenced by her Untransformed Life ante- and post- "belief"!

Again, what truly lies in DON's heart we cannot discern, but we can attest that anyone who lives an Untransformed Life is far more likely than not to the Logos declare "I know you not."

4.7 Confession of an American Pharisee

For the director of music. A psalm of David. When the prophet Nathan came to him after David had committed adultery with Bathsheba.

Have mercy on me, O God, according to your unfailing love; according to your great compassion blot out my transgressions. Wash away all my iniquity and cleanse me from my sin. For I know my transgressions, and my sin is always before me. Against you, you only, have I sinned and done what is evil in your sight, so that you are right in your verdict and justified when you judge. Surely I was sinful at birth, sinful from the time my mother conceived me. Surely you desire truth in the inner parts; you teach me wisdom in the inmost place. Cleanse

me with hyssop, and I will be clean; wash me, and I will be whiter than snow. Let me hear joy and gladness; let the bones you have crushed rejoice. Hide your face from my sins and blot out all my iniquity. Create in me a pure heart, O God, and renew a steadfast spirit within me. Do not cast me from your presence or take your Holy Spirit from me. Restore to me the joy of your salvation and grant me a willing spirit, to sustain me. Then I will teach transgressors your ways, so that sinners will turn back to you. Save me from the guilt of bloodshed, O God, you who are God my Savior, and my tongue will sing of your righteousness. Open my lips, Lord, and my mouth will declare your praise. You do not delight in sacrifice, or I would bring it; you do not take pleasure in burnt offerings. My sacrifice, O God, is a broken spirit; a broken and contrite heart you, God, will not despise. (Ps 51:1–17)
King David

Written as a mental health exercise, the following confession is from a Descendant of Noah who suffered from alcohol, gambling, and sex addictions. A courageous example of honest introspection, you will find it to be a helpful exposition of many of the subjects discussed in this handbook so far, including false practices, self-loathing, fellowship, and love. Note that the term "American" refers to a resident of Middle New Canaan.

I am an American Pharisee. I didn't recognize the similarities in my life to that of the biblical Pharisee until life circumstances forced me to look in the mirror. I was horrified to see the cold, naked truth staring back at me. I could no longer buy into the outward appearances that I conveyed to others and to myself. Instead of piety I saw hypocrisy. Instead of humility I saw pride. Instead of goodwill I saw prejudice. Instead of power I saw impotence. Instead of faith in God I saw faith in self.

I had spent a lifetime carefully protecting my blindness to these realities. I'm amazed with what skill and energy I fabricated an elaborate system of ruses to fool everyone, including myself, into thinking that I was a good and decent Christian. In college, I'd espouse love and tolerance every Tuesday at the Bible study I attended, while harboring resentments toward black men, "loose" women, gays, liberals, and just about anybody who was different from me. When I was a firefighter, I sang praises to God every Sunday in chapel and used his name in vain every weekday at the station. I led a teen fellowship every Wednesday evening where I often reminded my pupils of their spiritual duty to remain chaste; yet I was secretly using pornography.

The great promise of marriage (limitless and legitimate sex) motivated me to find a girl worth the pains of long-term dating and I found that girl in the form of the earthbound angel I met at church. I thought her simple honesty, genuine purity, and charming naïveté would save me from myself—that she could make me complete. I proposed and she accepted, and because she was a virgin (yes!) and she wanted to wait until we were married (no!), I had to use a little porn to get by until the wedding (well . . .).

The great promise of marriage turned out to be the great lie and before long I returned to paper girls and phone sex to meet the needs my wife ~~could~~ would not gratify. I hid my sordid secrets from my wife, leaving her to live in tortured confusion as she watched the man she thought she knew become progressively and inexplicably angry, sullen, and distant. I swore off sexual sins

Wo|Man: Nature & Nativity

week after week, year after year, sincerely believing my commitment each time. When our first child, a beautiful boy, was born I put down the magazines and hung up the phone forever!

With all my newfound free time, I purchased a 3200-Baud modem and figured out how to download pornographic pictures over this new titillating digital world called the Internet. All the while I portrayed the thoughtful, loving husband in public but I was an insensitive, irritable, self-centered, judgmental jackass at home and within my own thoughts. I was quick to judge others for what lay within me, consistently failing to hear the hypocrisy roll off my lips. I couldn't hear anything truthful over the din of my pride.

Throughout my days this pride has given voice to the guiding force of my ego. It tells me that I'm such a wonderful person I can't have any faults. So, naturally, if I dimly perceive any evidence of personal fault, I attack it, deny it, or run away. Actually, if you must know what I truly think: I'm not merely a wonderful person; I'm the best person. I'm better than everybody else, and if there's any endeavor in which I'm not the best, than it's not a worthy endeavor. To be perfectly candid, I'm not just the best person; I'm the only person. What's my evidence? Well, there's always me and there are people who come in and out of my life. My ego is aware of nothing else.

Do you think me crazy? I wonder how this must sound to the rational mind, which I'm only just now coming to know firsthand. You see, I have been crazy for most of my life. It's crazy for a teenage boy to feel compelled to continue to steal alcohol and dirty magazines after he's been arrested twice and risks time in "Juvie Hall" if caught again. It's crazy to cheat and plagiarize myself out of a college education that I took out a loan for! It's crazy to earnestly believe that the next girlfriend will make my life whole time after time after time. It's crazy to neglect and abuse close friendships, and then blame God for my insufferable loneliness. It's crazy to play computer games rather than read bedtime stories to my son, then surf the Web for porn until the wee hours of the morning while my wife sleeps alone in bed, and, a few hours later, sit at work exhausted and distracted, expecting my employer to reward me with a promotion that I believe I so richly deserve. It's crazy to swear off pornography every week for a decade truly believing each time that "this time is the last time." It's crazy to meet the woman of my dreams, father a healthy boy and then a brilliant baby girl, and crave only what God does not set on my table. It's crazy to think that God is okay with all of this; that he doesn't mind my mockery. It's crazy to think I can serve two masters at once.

The truth is I've served one master since childhood: the almighty me. I've enthroned myself on the seat of self-worship. Please don't misunderstand my form of hubris—I thought I was humble, of course, because all great people, well many great people, are humble. In fact, I was quite proud of my humility. You see, I thought of myself as your equal when the whole time I knew I was better (how self-effacing!). But the greatest thing about me, as I used to believe, was that I was self-sufficient. I could rely on my own strength for anything and it was by my own strength that I would prove to the world how great I am. I just needed tangible validation from the world (i.e., those people who came in and out of my life) of my greatness.

Wo|Man: Nature & Nativity

So earning credit from the world dominated my pursuits. I became a master manipulator, getting others to see my façade as a genuine representation of the whole structure. As long as others confirmed my abilities and accomplishments, I was okay, but if I suspected others didn't find me exceptionally gifted, I worried. If I suspected others found fault with me, I panicked. If I suspected anyone might find out who I really was (or wasn't), I unraveled.

No one would accept me if they knew the truth. Deep down, I knew I was a complete failure. I was a waste of sperm, like my father used to remind me. I was a worthless, hopeless, shameful, perverted, lying, cheating imposter, paranoid that some day "they'll find out the truth about me." I hated myself. I was beyond redemption and deserved to burn in hell, where I knew I was going. Even God couldn't help (or wouldn't, because God knows I asked).

Do you find my self-description unbelievable? Do you doubt that I could have possibly held all of those mutually exclusive beliefs simultaneously? Remember what else I told you: I was crazy.

Am I sane now? Yes, that's how I know I was crazy back then. What changed? In short, the consequences of my actions caught up to me and forced me to see my unreality. I was stripped of my blinders, my mufflers, my lenses, my filters, my diversions, my anesthetics, my denial. With nothing to shield me from the truth of my abject, spiritual poverty, I found the pain unbearable and, in an act of unprecedented desperation, I asked for help.

Two decades of experimentation with self-deliverance yielded nothing but futile, if not laughable, attempts to salvage the wreckage of my life. Now I was willing to seek strength without me-myself-and-I. I took a few detours with well intentioned but equally lost "guides," eventually landing in a strange Augustine fellowship. Its people came from all walks of life: doctors, carpenters, priests, agnostics, men, women, black, yellow, white, gay, straight, pretty, ugly, sharp, dull, young, old—all leveled and united by their self-induced suffering. I so desperately wanted to belong to a different group—any group but this one! These people whom I reluctantly but instantly recognized as peers were outcasts and sinners by any definition. A strange mix of horror and relief flooded the shallow reservoir of my heart as the realization hit me: I was home, at last.

This odd collection of wounded souls took me in, accepted me for who I am, and loved me without condition. They shared their lives with humbling honesty and inspiring courage. They were being transformed right before my eyes, enjoying freedom from shameful deeds, which, in some cases, made my own past look mild by comparison. If these people could make it, I knew I could. I certainly yearned to find a more palatable association, but until I had the fortune of finding one, I determined to keep coming back.

I felt like a prisoner released from the suffocating darkness of solitary confinement, blinded by the light of day, trusting the hands of others to lead me. I heeded their advice as best my heart would allow. I began practicing honesty and openness with other people for the first time in my life. I actually developed friendships, deep and intimate ones, with other men. Instead of using the phone to get a fix, I used it to call for help. I admitted daily, sometimes hourly, that I am powerless over my self-destructive desires and I therefore yield to an all-powerful God whom I never really knew.

To my amazement and befuddlement, I immediately let go of my most destructive behaviors. I struggled periodically with certain persistent behaviors, but it's fair, nonetheless, to characterize the change in my conduct as substantive, and before long I experienced benefits that had nothing to do with my original goals stopping my out-of-control behavior.

For instance, it occurred to me one day that I was walking fully upright. There was no physical explanation for what arrested years of slouching, because the explanation was emotional: I was no longer ashamed! Do you have any idea what it is like for a wretch such as me to walk down the street unashamed? It is like receiving back a precious childhood gift you lost hope of ever seeing again (e.g., my yellow "banana bike" that someone stole in junior high).

Without warning or even my consent, I was living. As much as that may seem all well and good from an objective perspective, I hadn't signed up for real life. I just wanted to stop doing the things I didn't want to do. No one told me I would have to start dealing with emotions (to name just one of many objections). For instance, I watched a "Lassie" rerun—the one where her foot gets caught in a bear trap—and balled my eyes out. I'm a former firefighter for crying out loud! On top of this newly discovered vulnerability to the dramatic arts (I cannot adequately describe how unsettling that was), I became vulnerable to all manner of intimidating (i.e., intimate) experiences, which beforehand I had so masterfully inoculated and anesthetized myself from enduring.

Sitting with my emotions, actually caring about others' problems, and continually taking responsibility for my own actions overwhelmed me. I had no experience to draw upon, and the one piece of advice that I didn't follow that might have helped me get through this was asking someone to be my sponsor in the fellowship. The uncharted waters of Reality terrified me, so I demanded to take control of the helm, the Captain obliged, and I immediately followed the sirens' song.

Quickly lost in booze and squiggle-TV (scrambled pornography on the "adult" cable channel), I floundered in the waters of self-pity, blame, and despair. I quickly graduated from squiggle-TV to lingerie catalogues to printed pornography to online pornography, while verbally abusing my wife and children, physically abusing the family dog, and depleting our life savings on phone sex, online gambling, and ill-advised online stock trading. My work suffered, my children acted out, and my wife questioned, suspected, yelled, cried, pleaded, and eventually called our pastor for an intervention. I responded by spending more time away from home with newfound "friends" (cruising streets of Boston's "Combat Zone" and patronizing its strip clubs).

During this time I rejected lifelines that came in the form of phone calls from friends in the fellowship. Seething with resentment and shame, I let messages of help pile up in my voicemail, preferring my closer and lifelong friend, isolation. Then my wife handed me divorce papers.

I never really considered that someday my wife might actually leave me, but then again, I never really considered the possibility that I might have to explain how she contracted gonorrhea. I had no lies or false promises to offer

Wo|Man: Nature & Nativity

her or me. She refused to let me even attempt to apologize. She walled off. She gathered what little strength and dignity she could muster, and she invited me to leave and never come back.

Words fail me as I recall those dark days. My heart mourns and yearns for the wife of my youth. She was the most beautiful soul I could ever hope to know. She lived for others, offering all she had to give. She expected precious little in return, but quietly pined for (my) love. She had a soft spot for the downtrodden, the neglected, the abused. She wanted so badly to rescue me, but oh my, sweet Darling, you can't rescue a drowning man who won't let go of the millstone.

To say I hit rock bottom is the only accurate way to describe it. I had two choices: wilt and die, or grasp the extended, ubiquitous hand of God. I didn't know what kind of life I might have left to live. I had lost everything. Continuing seemed pointless. I thought that at least if I die in an "accident," my wife and children would receive life insurance, which would help balance the scales. This need to balance the scales welled up from somewhere deep within me: I had to pay a few debts before checking out of this miserable life.

Acting on this odd notion that I must settle my accounts before closing them, I returned a call to a close friend from fellowship. As soon as I heard his warm, familiar voice, I let go of the millstone. At long last, I was ready. I bore my soul and he listened. Through my heaving sobs, he heard me, he accepted me, and by the wonderful grace of my inestimable God, he loved me.

The next step I took was to call my baby sister. I needed a place to stay, but more than that, I needed family. She took me in and, despite what I had done, never judged me. That night, curled in her lap on a hand-me-down family couch,

Bound, an Earth Walker's Handbook

I prayed to the God Whom I Hardly Knew. I never said a word. I just sobbed and sobbed in his and her presence. I sobbed for my wife, for my children, for myself, for my friends, for my brothers and my sister, for my Maker, for mercy, for love, for hope, for compassion, for unmerited grace, for complete insufficiency, for addictions that led me to loss, and yet, to hope.

A few weeks later I was let go from my job but I didn't choose to self-medicate. At the direction of my new sponsor (the same friend whom I called that fateful night), I relied on his "4Fs" (friends, family, fellowship, and faith) and started anew (he pointed out, by the way, that family can be family-of-choice, not necessarily family-of-birth). The doors of opportunity had closed to so many what-could-have-beens, but I discovered new doors to what-may-yet-be.

I landed a job (with benefits!) at a local Starbucks coffee shop, which was quite a blessing because, although it represented a sharp pay cut, it was just enough to put bread on the table and pay rent to a program friend I moved in with. Plus, the predictable schedule and inability to "take work home" allowed me to go to more meetings, make more program calls, start seeing a shrink, have visitation with my kids (and be their taxi driver as often as I could) and help my wife with mowing the grass and other handyman chores, which I never did when I lived there (plus I used my severance package to pay off our mortgage).

I joined a new church that is far less religious and far more authentic than any I've experienced before. I've rejoined old twelve-step meetings and even helped formed new ones. I've rekindled old friendships and, of course, made new ones. I've

Wo|Man: Nature & Nativity

reached out to my dad and we're starting to (awkwardly but earnestly) relate as two adults.

Thanks entirely to my Creator, I have been free, one day at a time, from all of my addictions for nearly a year (that may sound insignificant but for me it's more incredible a story than Moses parting the Red Sea). My table is set each day with a magnificent bounty that nourishes, sustains, and delights me. I know what it is to love and to be loved. I live unafraid of the future or the past, because presently I surrender to the will of my Master. I know so very little about this God of mine, but at least I now know him at all. I know he is sufficient. I know that through my weakness he is strong, and I know that he consistently goes through every trial with me. He doesn't stop the trials (still a point of contention with me) but he is faithful to never leave my side.

In this last year—well, over all these years—God has taught me tolerance, mercy, and understanding. I accept that which I once refused. I love those whom I once thought threatened me. I relate to that and those which and whom I once misunderstood.

I am no longer consumed with self; I am consumed with a desire to reach out to those who are still sick and suffering, and to continue to grow in my relationship with my Maker. I no longer pray that when I die I won't go to hell; now I thank God that I no longer choose to live in hell.

I have no more doubts about my salvation, my purpose, or my direction. I live in peace, confidence, and stability. My 4Fs sustain me in times of crisis, even when it's self-induced. I still reach for the helm from time to time, but I have enough support in place to keep me in check. I have not reconciled with my wife but perhaps someday . . . but if not, I can honestly say that it is a joy to live alone and not feel lonely. The gifts I receive daily represent the amazing abundance that is available to all (and one doesn't even have to hit rock bottom to receive them).

If my life ends today, I can say I die without present regrets. I am doing the best I can and if my life really did end today, it would end with a sweet coda: this morning I found a card in the mail written in the familiar, juvenile penmanship of my son: "Dear Dad, thanks for sending me the Narnia books. I saw the ~~furst~~ first movie two times already! I can't wait to read the book and mom said I should ask you to read it with me. What do you think? Have a nice day being the best beareesta in the whole world!"

I immediately called my sister and left an unintelligibly giddy message. Then I called my sponsor and to his misfortune he answered the phone and listened to me jabber on about my son, Narnia, bearistas, and such . . .

What a merciful God I know. I hope and pray to have my family back but I claim no entitlement to them or anyone or anything. I am just so deeply grateful for what God has given me, what he has taken away, and what he has left me with.

Anonymous DON

Section 5

Controvert

*Let us examine some
common points of confusion.*

5.1 Mortal Fear: Good, Bad, or Indifferent?

MORTAL FEAR, SUCH A foreign emotion, is the subject of much controversy and debate during each COTC cycle and confounds many a trainee. Here are a few observations on this subject from those of the Long Earthen Line who have gone before you.

Human fear is not morally bad or good. Fear is an emotion, not an action, and therefore is categorized by MHS3 as amoral. Fear is not, however, insignificant.

As with all of DON's emotions, e.g., guilt and passion, fear can both benefit and harm its bearer and, in and of itself, we cannot classify it as either good or bad, even when its source is the First himself.

> What are fears but voices airy?
> Whispering harm where harm is not;

Bound, an Earth Walker's Handbook

> And deluding the unwary
> Till the fatal bolt is shot![1]
> William Wordsworth, poet,
> Hreyisles (GG), 634.805 to 664.025 AH

The morality of the matter, if one must phrase it that way, is how the subject of fear chooses to react. Specifically, does DON react to fear by running toward or away from her Maker & Redeemer? Incidentally, when dealing directly with a charge, an Earth Walker should avoid dragging her through questions of "morality"; rather, lead her to consider how the decisions before her may lead away or toward the Logos.

DON's reaction to fear propels her along the spiritual continuum with isolation at one end and communion at the other, the former bearing consumption and the latter bearing Preservation. While Real-beings clearly see the skirmish lines pushing and pulling along the spiritual continuum, human beings do not. Despite the clamor of battle raging about her, the illusions of the First's domain deafens DON to the spiritual forces that struggle toward isolation on the one wing and to toward communion on the other. She is not, however, impervious to the emotional effects of spiritual combat, the most prominent of which is fear. It is the duality of the source of fear that confuses DON; thus, our role is to help DON distinguish the fears-to-flee from the fears-to-pursue.

> You gain strength, courage, and confidence by every experience in which you really stop to look fear in the face. . . . The danger lies in refusing to face the fear.[2]
> Eleanor Roosevelt, activist and diplomat,
> New Canaan, 676.443 to 704.933 AH

---

1. Wordsworth, *Poetical Works*, 633.
2. Roosevelt, *Learn by Living*, 29.

Controvert

DON's confusion, of course, we owe to the *BOO!* who twist her fragile mind so that she runs away from such fears as trust, optimism, dissimilitude, and intimacy; yet runs toward mendacity, pessimism, intolerance, and loneliness. We realize this sounds ridiculous in the abstract, but not if you consider what you have witnessed from the watching vantages. How many times have you watched DON flee the wife of his youth; yet pursue the wife of his neighbor? DON fears both the healthy and the harmful connection—it is the sorting of what direction to run that continually trips her up.

5.2 Music: Good, Bad, or Indifferent?

Another common subject of debate and misunderstanding during Boot Camp is music. Heretofore you likely have never heard music from a source other than Choral Services, but now in Orientation Phase you have been subjected to the music of wo|man and you are undoubtedly dumbfounded to discover it is replete with blasphemies, hatred, self-aggrandizement, degradation of women, glorification of violence, and self-destruction. You will have also noted her music is insufficiently filled with affirmations, love, humility, respect, peace, and Preservation. It follows, therefore, that wo|mankind's music, on the whole, is harmful to the listener—correct?

Actually, we find the opposite to be true: generally music promotes fellowship, piques spiritual curiosity, and places the listener in the present. These three positive notes drown out, on the whole, the admittedly harmful impact of negative lyrics.

Music, a finite corollary to Infinite Mathematics, stimulates DON's body, mind, and soul. DON often cannot help but tap her foot, bob her head, smile or frown, laugh or cry, ponder, reflect, wonder, and connect. This feeling is akin to spiritual elevation from finite to Infinite, whetting the soul of the listener for what lies beyond her mortal existence.

> The thing that I think is interesting about both music and religion is that there's one thing that both share: the feeling of achieving transcendence. It's a hard word to understand, a difficult place to get to. You have to feel completely connected to the world and yourself, but at the same time be willing to be liberated from the world and from yourself.[3]
>
> Yo-Yo Ma, virtuoso,
> New Canaan, 702.376 to ExTBA AH

Lyrical songs, especially those that express sentiments listeners identify with, ignite DON's awareness of and longing for unity with fellow wo|man and with all Creation. Vocal harmonies compound this effect, often evoking a visceral compulsion to sing along, and DON's participation in a joyous (if not always pleasant) noise is the one of the closest experiences she can have to the communion we all know within the Infinite Dominion—to be one as we are one.

Music speaks directly to DON's soul (e.g., David's harp soothing Saul's tormented soul) and sparks spiritual spelunking, and we prefer any spiritual activity, regardless of the source or even the direction, over continued spiritual dormancy. As Lawrence Peter Berra, sportsman and humorist/philosopher, New Canaan, 691.418 to ExTBA AH, said, "When you come to a fork in the road, take it."[4]

Lastly and most importantly, music anchors the listener in the present—it cannot be experienced any other way! Whereas we can spend fruitless Guardian-hours trying to lead our charges into the present tense, immediately

---

3. Ma, "Big Interview," para. 26.
4. Berra, *Yogi Book*, 48.

Controvert

music can snatch DON from the past or future and land her flap-dab in the here-and-now.

As you are learning, DON commonly misses the opportunity of now to connect with her Maker & Redeemer, preoccupied with dwelling on the past or worrying about the future. Music is an efficacious tool to place her in the present, and as such, we encourage aspiring Earth Walkers to consider music as a tool to aid in the development of our mortal charges.

5.3 Organized Religion: Good, Bad, Indifferent?

Perhaps the most controversial subject we cover in COTC is organized religion; even within the senior ranks of Guardian Services opinions are divided. Those in favor of organized religion cite spiritual benefits such as fellowship, worship, and corporate prayer. Those against it cite spiritual hazards such as homogeneity, intolerance, and externalism.

MHS3's official diagnosis is that organized religion on Earth suffers from social schizophrenia. Witness from the watching vantages the bifurcated symptoms in New Canaan such as teaching their children and abusing their children, or feeding the poor outside the church and robbing the poor inside the church, or protecting rights and taking rights. Historically speaking, the organized religions in New Canaan have a similarly schizophrenic record: living peacefully with the indigenous nations and destroying the indigenous nations, fighting slavery and protecting slavery, freeing the Judiachs from "concentration camps" and placing the Jyaponisha into "internment camps."

> In the so-called Ages of Faith, when men really did believe the Christian religion in all its

Bound, an Earth Walker's Handbook

> completeness, there was the inquisition, with its tortures; there were millions of unfortunate women burned as witches. . . . You will find as you look around the world that every single bit of progress in humane feeling, every improvement in criminal law, every step toward the diminution of war, every step toward better treatment of the colored races, or every mitigation of slavery, every moral progress . . . has been consistently opposed by the organized churches of the world.[5]
>
> Bertrand Russell, philosopher,
> Hreyisles (GG), 672.060 to 707.856 AH

Given the dichotomous impact of organized religion on wo|man, do we throw out the fledgling with the baptism water? By no means! The body of the Logos, a.k.a. the church, can manifest itself quite authentically through organized religion. The key to achieving this lofty goal is reducing (ideally eliminating) the influence of individual wo|men and growing (ideally installing) the influence of the Ghost of God.

The sole reason organized religions and their churches fail on any account is the impact of their own, flawed, mortal leadership. Given DON's inclination within hierarchical organizations to substitute God's direction with her own, we seldom observe the sovereignty of God the Founder at the level of religious orders and divisions. We do, on the other wing, witness the active leadership of God's Ghost at the level of individual churches, both within and without larger religious organizations.

Such healthy churches thrive by surrendering their will to the direction of God the Founder as communicated by his Ghost. This is not easily achieved for it requires trust—not merely individually but corporately. It was one

---

5. Russell, *Not a Christian*, 20–21.

Controvert

thing for Simon Peter to briefly walk on water but true collective faith would have the entire crew and passengers step out onto the unknown!

Extensive research in this field conducted by MHS3 shows that churches and otherwise religiously linked groups that truly walk on water* share a number of common attributes:

- Deferent. They yield to the will of God.

- Mutual Respect. Members or parishioners share a respect for one another. They do not interrupt others while they are speaking; in fact, they actually listen to one another. They do not judge one another; in fact, they affirm one another.

- Safe. Members or parishioners uphold the principles of love and honor so that all feel safe to be themselves without fear.

- Flexible yet Grounded. They constantly adapt practices to meet changing conditions yet they honor tradition; for example, they may dispense with sermons (halleluiah) in favor of group discussion yet maintain certain liturgies of their particular heritage.

- Organizationally Flat. Generally, the healthiest religious organizations are the least organized.

- Egalitarian. Congregants enjoy equal social status, from priest to parishioner.

- No Great Men. A healthy church lacks mortal heroes—those living legends in whom DON can misplace her faith; rather, clergy and other leadership strive not to be noticed, directing all attention to God the Founder.

- Rotational Leadership. Clerical leadership changes cyclically in order to ensure the church is a reflection of the Shepard, not its pastor.

- Genuine. As a body they share an ethos of earnestness. Individually, each is free to be authentic.
- Humble and Open. Parishioners share and own their shortcomings to not only heal but to connect with others who suffer similarly.
- Involved. They marshal the collective power of their fellowship to make a difference in their community through clothing drives, library donations, medical donations, soup kitchens, prison ministries, home building, and the like.
- Trust over Fear. They overcome their fears of the unknown and place faith in the Ghost to express itself through the collective body of their church/group.
- Tempered Tolerance. They welcome diverse and even challenging opinions tempered by mutual respect and safety. They will, for example, listen without prejudice to a member who challenges a core tenant of faith but, on the other wing, will immediately intervene when a member disparages another.
- Balanced Boundaries. Members or parishioners respect one another's boundaries. They provide an ear to a fellow's troubles but refrain from proffering advice unless invited to do so. They honor privacy in most cases but will collectively intervene when someone's actions "scream" for help (e.g., addiction). When a person, inside or outside the fellowship, loses a loved one to the Angel of Death, members will render practical aid such as childcare, food, and quiet presence, and forgo sharing opinions, advice, and platitudes.
- Witness by Action More than Words. DON espouses that actions speak louder than words but she seldom

applies this to her religious and spiritual convictions. Healthy churches and fellowships do not find lost sheep by talking but by searching. They do not nourish the hungry with parchment but with grain. They do not heal the sick through oration but through treatment.

> I needed clothes and you clothed me, I was sick and you looked after me, I was in prison and you came to visit me. (Matt 25:36)
> Jyeshua

As one should expect under entropic governance (see 6.1: Order of Realities), there are many variations and combinations of healthy churches but they do generally share a majority of the aforementioned attributes. The best examples we find are non-divisional, independent, and relatively small religious groups and churches, but that is by no means to the exclusion of larger, more traditional organizations.

If healthy churches as described above cannot be found proximate to a charge, should a CO encourage her to dispense with church and fellowship altogether? We suggest that the answer to this question depends upon the immediate and unique needs of a charge.

As DON matures socially, she generally trends from subjectivity toward objectivity. If a charge sees herself exclusively or predominantly from her own perspective and she is unable or has great difficulty "putting herself in someone else's sandals," then push her toward a local Jyeshuan church and other socially constructive organizations or groups—she needs the experiences these settings provide to mature. If, on the other wing, she sees herself fairly objectively and is capable of empathy, she will be better off on her own than in the company of a dysfunctional religious body.

There is much more to discuss on this matter and undoubtedly some lively debates await you during Academic Phase. Until then, mull our comments herein.

* Note: DON commonly misinterprets the example of "walking on water" to mean perfection, rather than faith.

5.4 Proper Government

The proper form of government for wo|man during the Age of Harvest has been a source of disagreement for most COTC cycles. To prepare the discussion, it helps to establish the impact of government on the spiritual health of wo|man. Recall Israel, and Judah in her wake, building idols in the shape of calves and Asherah poles on the high places, bowing down to the suns of welkin and to Grand Marshal Baal, sacrificing their children by fire, practicing Majikk, and selling themselves to the powers of the First. Now, in the Age of Harvest, gaze upon the high towers built to Marshal Mammon, from Mayiya to New Canaan to Greater Gothika to the Hardlands to India to Persia to Center Earth—all raised in the name of greed, exploitation, and personal wealth beyond means to consume. Peer upon the twain towers that burned to the ground in Bala Ledd where religious and worldly fanaticism (two heads of the same Beast) collided. In all of these circumstances you will discover the direct relationship between a leader's spiritual health and those of her pupils, citizens, and disciples.

Throughout extent scriptures we see the proclamations of the King affected the entire nation of Israel (e.g., King Zedekiah). Take this principle down a level or so, and you will find the actions of any mortal leader affect the spiritual welfare of her subjects, subordinates, and servants.

Controvert

> An institution is the lengthened shadow of one man; as, Monachism, of the Hermit Antony; the Reformation, of Luther; Quakerism, of Fox; Methodism, of Wesley; Abolition, of Clarkson.[6]
> Ralph Waldo Emerson, poet and writer,
> New Canaan, 646.858 to 675.713 AH

This tight relationship of leader to led is an ever present source of ruin for the Descendants of Noah under all but the theocratic form of government we saw during the leadership of the Judges.

In the Age of the Fall and the Age of Stagnation leadership went to the strong, which is often, but not always, a failing proposition given the strong tend to exploit the weak. During the Age of Theophany, leadership of Israel was deferred to the religious prelates and judges; this was the golden age of human governance before wo|man's demands for kings and demagogues, the birth of aristocracy, the rise of pagan popularism (usually plutocracies masquerading as democracies), and the pernicious, ever-present growth of oligarchies.

Given this poor selection of governance for contemporary wo|man, some of us prefer the monarchy. Guardians who argue this perspective tout at least by chance DON will have a greater percentage of benevolent leaders than by the popularly chosen governors of most "civilized" nations in this age.

Those of us who disagree point out that, given the extraordinary power of the monarch, the destruction caused by a despot far outweighs the prosperity fostered by a beneficent sovereign, and history shows the vast majority of monarchs tend to prosper themselves at the expense of their citizens.

> Really, that men born to a throne (limited or unlimited) should employ the brief span of their

---

6. Emerson, "Self-Reliance," 62.

> existence here in doing all the mischief in their power, in levying cruel wars and undermining the liberties of the world, to prove to themselves and others that their pride and passions are of more consequence than the welfare of mankind at large, would seem a little astonishing, but that the fact it is so.[7]
>
> William Hazlitt, writer,
> Hreyisles (GG), 637.727 to 656.720 AH

Should we therefore trust popularism, a.k.a. the rule of the people? By no means! If the will of the people governed Israel at the dawn of the Age of Theophany, would Moses have led his people out of the wilderness, let alone out of bondage in Egypt? In its modern nursery, did not popularism abet the displacement and destruction of indigenous nations and the abduction and enslavement of the peoples of Lesser Sheba and Greater Ghana?

Furthermore, wo|mankind's practice of popularism rarely achieves its espoused purpose: rule of the people. Nominally in charge, the nugatory 99 percent of nationals forfeit power to the 1 percent of plutocrats who surpass even a prince's proclivity to prosper personally via privation of the populace.

Could wo|man return to the leadership of judges? We have not observed this form of governance in the Age of Harvest but we suspect it is nonetheless possible. The problem, of course, is how would wo|man empanel the ruling bench? The answer is only by direction of the Logos, and such guidance will only be proffered when a nation, as a whole, seeks its Maker & Redeemer. Recall how Judge Gideon replied to the Israelites when they pleaded for him to rule over them: "I will not rule over you, nor will my son rule over you. The Lord will rule over you" (Judg 8:23).

---

7. Hazlitt, "Monarchy," 315.

Controvert

Given the piteous state of humanity's spiritual health, especially as nation-states, a return to judges is hardly plausible.

Is there no viable form of self-governance for our motley mortals? Indeed there is. We submit and suggest the matriarchal monarchy. By enthroning solely the female of the species, humanity would dramatically reduce the probability of tyrannical rule to an acceptable minimum, and yet enjoy the benefits of the most effective form of self-governance (apart from divine direction). Monarchies, however, are going the way of Giants as we approach End Times and will soon be extinct in favor of pagan popularism.

Wherefore our most productive course of action is to encourage DON to exclude males from executive and legislative public office—at least at the national level. We recommend continuance of men's suffrage and even holding some forms of local political office, but any measure of reason would not grant them significant authority over fellow citizens and never empower them to declare war (to be clear, men can wage war, they just should not start them). That men are naturally tyrannical and violent is a matter of historical record and biological composition, just as women are naturally nurturing and irenic.

> . . . by the way, in the new Code of Laws which I suppose it will be necessary for you to make I desire you would Remember the Ladies, and be more generous and favourable to them than your ancestors. Do not put such unlimited power into the hands of the Husbands. Remember all Men would be tyrants if they could. . . . That your Sex are Naturally Tyrannical is a Truth so thoroughly established as to admit of no dispute.[8]
> Abigail Adams, Queen Mother,
> New Canaan, 625.308 to 652.337 AH

---

8. Adams, *Letters*, 147.

This brings us back to the critical points made in 3.1: Boxing Gold; 3.7: The Wrong Government; and 2.5: Communion; namely, DON needs to focus on the Kingdom of God, on her relationship to her Maker & Redeemer, and on her fellowship with other persons. Only then, and only by inadvertent consequence, will a suitable form of self-government become possible.

In conclusion, countries, communities, compacts, communes, collectives, and corporations all reflect the principal principles of their leaders. The course of human events can be permanently affected by the decisions of a few. Those best able to govern are not the most prominent, educated, intelligent, or charismatic; rather, they are the ones who seek God. If, by Providence, you are assigned a charge who seeks or has secured political assignment, it is your incumbent duty to convey to your charge the best way to bear that responsibility: focus her energies on her faith foremost.

5.5 Castrate the Creator?

Most men and women hold the impudent notion that the Creator has a sex. The multifarious reasons for this misconception include male dominance of most human societal structures (derived from the relative physical strength of men over women), the first creation story of man in our own image (yes, they believe we are sexed as well), the disproportional representation of men in extent scriptures (Judge Deborah and Mary the Mother of Jyeshua notwithstanding), Saul-Paul's erroneous admonition against women speaking on holy ground, and the exclusive record of Real-beings appearing as men in extent scriptures.*

While it would be healthy to disabuse our charges of the myth of a sexed Divinity, DON's visceral response to such attempts discourages us from trying in most cases. If you are not familiar with this peeve of Jyeshuans, refer to the Founder as "her" or "it" and watch your charge's nostrils flare, jugular veins swell, and vision narrow. She cannot hear another word you say and will likely write you off permanently for stirring up this peculiarly unwelcome subject.

The unfortunate consequence of the myth of divine gender is the spiritually superior sex has been effectually silenced throughout the history of "mankind"; not to mention the egregious suffering women have endured at the hands of chauvinism. Additionally, DON's perspective of the Founder is skewed toward male attributes such as strength and conviction but lacks female attributes such as nurture and forbearance.

> Oh God, why wasn't I born a male so that my every desire would be to serve you, to do right in all things, and to be perfect a creature as man claims to be?[9]
> Christine de Pizan, poet and writer,
> Greater Gothika, 486.513 to 510.620 AH

A more balanced understanding of Divinity and of themselves would certainly improve the spiritual health of our charges, and though yet a distant vision, it is certainly not far beyond the horizon. In fact, as twilight settles on the Age of Harvest we detect a favorable cline across the nations toward acceptance of the Feminine Holy. Nonetheless, we still do not advocate castrating your charges' Creator; just encourage a balanced view of our genderless Creator when you encounter open doors through which to do so.

*Male corporeal form is preferred by Messenger Services because DON is predisposed, and therefore far more receptive, to listen to "men." GS COs, on the other wing,

---

9. Pizan, *City of Ladies*, 4.

Bound, an Earth Walker's Handbook

prefer female corporeal form for it reduces our risk of detection by DON.

5.6 Scriptures, Canon, Apocrypha, and the Like

The critical context to examine the subject of scriptures, canon, apocrypha, and the like is the fallibility of the steward of such documents: wo|man. Why is this obvious fact critical? Because, particularly in the New Canaan AOR, both Reversionist and Universal Jyeshuans esteem their extent scriptures (which, by the flight, vary between the two divisions) to be infallible. Some Reversionist subdivisions go so far as to make this perspective an article of faith with implications for parishioner Preservation.

The hazards of this misguided belief include a propensity toward externalism, religious myopia, squandered attention on study versus communion, deference to the written canon over the still small voice of God's Ghost, a limited and skewed knowledge of God the Founder, a closed-mind to God "outside the box," intolerance and fear and persecution of diversity, diminution of women, and justification of human slavery—just to name a few.

Should COs therefore encourage charges to disregard their scriptures? By no means! Extent scriptures contain the word of God; we just need to caution DON that the law of God is also written in her heart and when what she reads wars against what she knows she should meditate and pray for discernment, keeping the whole of her Bible as context for any text in question.

How is it that Jyeshuans believe their scriptures are without error? MHS3 informs us there are three primary reasons. First, when Jyoe average Jyeshuan considers questioning scripture, she suffers a paralyzing panic attack believing if she finds one flaw, then the entirety of her Bible

Controvert

will unravel destroying her faith along with it. This irrational fear keeps most from entertaining any scrutiny of the canon whatsoever.

Secondly, Jyeshuans cling to scriptural infallibility for the same reason DON prefers external guidance over individual moral decision making—it is far easier because it relieves DON of personal responsibility. If DON must discern truth, she realizes that she becomes responsible for her decisions and actions. If, on the other wing, she acts solely on the authority of external sources (e.g., the Bible), she believes she cannot be held responsible.

Thirdly, Jyeshuan adherents to scriptural infallibility (a.k.a. inerrantists) do not know, or at least understand, the content of their holy cannon because it is impossible for any sentient being of mediocre intelligence to comprehend the Bible and yet believe it to be without error. As Thom Stark, author and filmmaker, New Canaan, 711.872 to ExTBA AH reveals, "There are those who *claim* to be inerrantists. There are those who *think* that they are inerrantists. But in truth, nobody is really an inerrantist." He expounds:

> It would be difficult to find an inerrantist who believed that Ashur, Ashera, Marduk, and Kemosh were real gods in ancient Near East; equally difficult to find an inerrantist who believed that when Yahweh was a young deity he received the land of Israel as an inheritance from his father, the mountain god of El Elyon ... that, according to the Bible, Yahweh not only desired, but commanded and expected Israelites to sacrifice their children ... that it is morally acceptable even to own a slave, let alone to beat that slave.[10]

10. Stark, *Faces*, 15–16.

If this makes no sense to you, you are not alone and, blessedly, understanding the befuddling bipolar bent of an inerrantist is purely a luxury. What is essential is that Delta Team members know the nature of the Jyeshuan canons and encourage charges to consider their scriptures with their conscience as guided by the Ghost of God.

How did the modern Jyeshuan canons come about? It is a complex story and the subject of an entire course you will take in Academic Phase; the Saint Mark version of the story goes something like this:

- The Descendants of Adam lacked written communication. To their posterity they passed on oral histories such as Eden, the fall, antediluvian times, the flood, the spread of nations, and Abraham.

- Moses, with contributions from scribes and priests, recorded much of the aforementioned history as well as Israel's captivity, exodus from Egypt, the wilderness, the tablets, Bezalel's ark, the ordination of Aaron, laws and regulations, Israel's apostasy, the commission of Jyoshua, and the death of Moses.

- Prophets, historians, and witnesses, as well as false prophets and imposters, compiled texts over the ensuing millennia—some heavily inspired by God; some not inspired at all; some preserved and passed down in approximate original form; some preserved and passed down significantly altered; and some lost or destroyed by wo|men or by the physical laws of the 666th Realm.

- Judiach clerics and scribes, influenced by the Ghost of God and by their own faculties, settled on a common canon shortly before the Advent of Jyeshua (there was disagreement over the canonicity of seven "books" but the formation of the old canon was otherwise concluded).

Controvert

- Witnesses to the Penultimate Theophany recorded their memories and knowledge of Jyeshua with some diversity but overall with preponderant commonality. Many but not all of these witness records survived the passage of time including the development of a new canon by leaders of the infant Jyehsuan religion.

- Subsequent to the death and resurrection of Jyeshua, apostles spread his words and recorded their acts and beliefs. Some of these records—the aforementioned theophanic witness accounts, apostolic letters, and visions—began to emerge as the new canon (both instead of and in addition to the old canon).

- Several clerical declarations, written opinions, and corporate reviews of canon, consisting of the now combined old and new canons, were conducted in the second, fourth, eighth, and fifteenth centuries YOW. These resulted in the combined universal Jyeshuan canon, which DON took to be the final canon until the Reversionist Movement.

- Under the leadership of Martin Luther, cleric and scribe, Greater Gothika, 529.978 to 552.989 AH, the Reversionists challenged, among other things, the combined universal canon and revised it in the sixteenth century YOW by removing the seven old canon books in question and categorizing them as hidden books (using the Greco rubric "apocrypha" first coined by Jerome, Jyeshuan prelate, Palatine (GG), 115.054 to 141.717 AH). Martin Luther also removed four new canon books and categorized them as less than canonical. The Universalists, by the flight, did not take kindly to said revisions, leading, in part, to thirty years of war throughout Greater Gothika wherein Jyeshuans slaughtered one another in the name of God.

- Subsequent Reversionist leaders agreed to reinstate the four new canon books Martin Luther removed but decided to do away with the seven old canon apocryphal books altogether, resulting in a total of sixty-six "books" (this numerical signpost, blatantly human though it is, still goes without notice).

The point of this 30,000-cubit-high view of canon development is that fallible "man" played the central role in the development and maintenance of Universalist and Reversionist Holy Scripture. In light of this fact and its implications, have we not encouraged Jyeshuan DON to question her canon?

Yes indeed. We have repeatedly broached this subject over the centuries but most Jyeshuans erupt in panicked terror believing that any crack in the façade of scriptural infallibility will tear down the whole structure of their faith. Not surprisingly, we consistently encounter the same type of vehement and visceral response encountered when one introduces DON to the notion of God's femininity.

Unlike the subject of the Feminine Holy, however, pushing DON to recognize the limitations and flaws of her canon is critical to her willingness to directly meet her Maker & Redeemer. If she believes, as many do, that all she needs is the "Good Book," she becomes vulnerable to spiritual false practices such as legalism, externalism, believism, and cognition—all deadly surrogates of the Logos. Likewise, complacent reliance on her Bible dulls her spiritual awareness and senses, thereby diminishing her desire to develop a personal relationship with her Maker & Redeemer and even her ability to recognize him.

Do we therefore encourage our charges to disregard their scriptures? By no means! Extent scriptures contain the word of God; we just need to caution DON that the law of God is also written in her heart and when what she reads

Controvert

wars against what she knows, she should meditate and pray for discernment, keeping the whole of her Bible as context for any text in question.

> I do not feel obliged to believe that the same God who has endowed us with sense, reason, and intellect has intended us to forgo their use.[11]
> Galileo Galilei, astronomer,
> Greater Gothika, 559.563 to 588.053 AH

How do we help DON to see her canon objectively? First, we encourage her overcome her fear of using her faculties to critically examine the texts she considers holy. Second, we adduce the most obvious failings of extent scriptures. Here is a small sampling (for the purpose of representation, not persuasion) from the contemporary Reversionists' unofficially approved translation of the Holy Scripture, a.k.a. the 1984 edition of the New International Version (NIV) Holy Bible, which you will examine in full detail during Academic Phase:

- Judges 9:22–23. "After Abimelech had governed Israel three years, God sent an evil spirit between Abimelech and the citizens of Shechem God." This assertion is not only false; it is blasphemous. Using the whole of her Bible as context for the text in question, let us consider: "You are not a God who takes pleasure in wickedness; nor shall evil dwell with you" (Tehillim 5:4); "You are of purer eyes than to behold evil, and cannot look on wickedness" (Book of Habakkuk 1:13); "When tempted, no one should say, 'God is tempting me.' For God cannot be tempted by evil, nor does he tempt anyone" (Book of Jyames 1:13); "God is light; in him there is no darkness at all" (1 Jyahn 1:5). God never has and never will dispatch evil forces; the

11. Galilei, "Letter," 183.

aforementioned verse in Judges is errant.

- We find this same blasphemy repeated in the Book of Jyoshua 23:15 and 1 Samuel 16:14. In the latter, a mortal reader of average aptitude would realize that for God to send an evil spirit into King Saul, God would be collaborating with the enemy in an effort to destroy David! This lie slipped into DON's cannon at the hands of the actual dispatcher of Saul's demon—the fallen First himself. If we look at the whole of her Bible as context for the text in question we find, among other things, that "Satan rose up against Israel and incited David to take a census" (1 Chronicles 21:1). This is a true statement and ascribes blame appropriately to the Master of Malfeasance.

- In 1 Samuel 15:29 we read, "He who is the Glory of Israel does not lie or change his mind; for he is not a man, that he should change his mind." This is also incorrect; God the Founder can and does change his mind. Again, turning to the context of text we can examine Exodus 32:9–14; 2 Kings 20:1–6; Jonah 3:10, and several others to readily see that God the Founder is not limited; rather, he is able and willing to change direction as he deems appropriate.

- In the Book of Jude 1:14–15 we find a quotation from a non-canonical source: "Enoch, the seventh from Adam, prophesied about these men: 'See, the Lord is coming with thousands upon thousands of his holy ones to judge everyone, and to convict all the ungodly of all the ungodly acts they have done in the ungodly way, and of all the harsh words ungodly sinners have spoken against him.'" Turning to Jude's source, the Book of Enoch, which Reversionists and Universalists deem unconfirmed and uninspired pseudo-scripture, we find the referenced passage: "And behold! He cometh with ten thousands of his holy ones to execute judgment upon all, and to destroy all the ungodly: and to convict all flesh of all the works of their ungodliness which they have ungodly committed, and of all the hard things which ungodly sinners have spoken against him."[12] How can the Book of Jude be an infallible, God-breathed scripture yet reference hearsay heresy as truth? It cannot, and since the Book of Enoch is pseudo-scripture (by the flight, we verified with Enoch that he wrote no such document—in fact, he reports he was illiterate until joining us in the Dominion), the Book of Jude is either contaminated or entirely pseudo-scripture as well.

- Acts of the Apostles 1:18 mistakenly reports that Judas Iscariot died by spontaneous abdominal eruption; whereas he actually hanged himself (Gospel of Matthew 27:5).

- Gospel of Jyahn 1:18 and 1 Timothy 6:16 inform us that "No man hath seen God at any time" or can see God. Although potentially fatal to a mortal, it is possible to see God the Founder as accurately recorded in Genesis 32:30 and Exodus 33:11: "For I have seen God face to face, and my life is preserved"; "And the Lord spake to Moses face to face, as a man speaketh to his friend."

Are the particular scriptures, or books, mentioned above largely corrupted, tainted, or otherwise suspect? No, these works on the whole reflect the truth of DON's history and the Truth of God's word. Are there scriptures included in the Reversionist Jyeshuan canon that are largely tainted or even errantly included? Indeed there are. Peruse the

12. *Book of Enoch*, 2.

Song of Solomon and you will immediately agree without need for further explanation. DON, ironically, is too afraid of blasphemy to state the obvious blasphemy of including this titillating work in the canon.

If the current canon is incomplete, are there lost scriptures that should be included in the canon? We can state there are lost scriptures that could be included in the canon, such as Chronicles of the Kings of Media and Persia, the Book of Giants, and the First Epistle to the Ephesians. Whether they should be included in the extent canon, however, is solely the agency of the Founder, Ghost & Logos.

Given the errors and omissions of extent scriptures should we therefore encourage our charges to disregard their scriptures? By no means! Extent scriptures contain the word of God; we just need to caution DON that the law of God is also written in her heart and when what she reads wars against what she knows, she should meditate and pray for discernment, keeping the whole of her Bible as context for any text in question.

5.7 In His Name

Iza'ah, Jyahn, Jyeshua, and others in extent scriptures decree the efficacy of praying and believing in the name of the Logos—and rightfully so! The problem you will encounter on Earth is that DON takes this literally. DON presumes she actually knows The Name That Cannot Be Known. Furthermore, DON believes that her Preservation is staked upon use of the penultimate theophanic name ascribed to the incarnate Maker & Redeemer in Judea, rather than upon use of his True Name. More vexing, DON does not use the historically accurate name Jyeshua, citing instead dialectical derivations such as Jeezus, Heyzeus, and Yoshua to name a select few.

Controvert

All this would be of little concern to us if it did not result in the tragic alienation of countless souls. For example, if a child of God knows the Logos, and yet refers to him as "Gwhop," a New Canaan Jyeshuan will likely inform this child that she is condemned unless she starts pronouncing The Name That Cannot Be Known as "Jeezus."

New Canaan Jyeshuans cling to this nearly universal misunderstanding despite the potential horrific consequences:

- Jyeshuans can bully those who do not express the Logos exactly as they do.
- Jyeshuans can deceive themselves that they know their Maker & Redeemer merely on the basis of pronunciation.
- Jyeshuans can ostracize themselves from their fellow wo|man by claiming exclusive gnosis of God.

If the efficacy of praying and believing in the Name of God is not based on pronunciation, what is it based on? AA Raphael advises us it is based on knowing the God Who Preserves. When DON reaches her wit's end, realizes her insufficiency, and reaches out to the God Who Preserves, immediately she meets her Maker & Redeemer. The Ancient of Days will choose to reveal himself as he sees fit—perhaps as a brilliant fire alighting a bush, a wheel within a wheel, or a beaten man hanging upon a cross. The key point to impress upon your charges is that God's revelations will vary but his identity does not. It is up to DON to search beyond a historical holy manifestation in order to meet, know, and grow in her personal knowledge and relationship with the Maker & Redeemer as he chooses to reveal himself today.

The confusion surrounding this subject stems from Jyeshua's life, death, and resurrection. Modern Jyeshuans understand the fundamental truth that all hope of mortal Preservation for Eternity was and is staked upon the cross; however, they interpolate knowing the Maker & Redeemer with knowledge of the Penultimate Theophany. Ignoring that her Bible reveals that Moses and Elijah survived their mortal expirations, Jyeshuans dismiss that wo|man can meet the Logos without learning about the historical Nazarene. Most troublesome, some Jyeshuans replace knowing the God Who Preserves with knowing of the Nazarene, thereby unwittingly rejecting the Grace of God and its attendant Preservation!

Faith is not based on a third-party introduction to a historical persona who by definition does not exist; rather, faith is based on direct and intimate interaction with the God Who Is, the great *I Am*.

Therefore encourage your charges to abjure their beliefs that they must know The Name That Cannot Be Known and that those who pronounce the name differently cannot possibly know the same God. Your charges merely need to seek, meet, and know their Maker & Redeemer. Accordingly, focus them on the Kingdom of God, for therein they will find the Prince of Peace, by whose name they are preserved without ever knowing it.

Section 6

Finite Realm 666

Prepare yourself for the physical realm.

6.1 Order of Realities

To FRAME OUR DISCUSSION of Finite Realm 666 herein, we shall refer to AA Michael's Order of Realities as outlined below:

Eternity—Subreality
- Eternal Void of origin and destination
- Singularity of consciousness
- Dimensionless
- Mathematic Governance

Infinity—Reality
- Progeny of the Void
- Sum of consciousness
- Dozen-dimensioned
- Dominion of Divinity
- Domain of Holy Host
- Holy Governance

Finite Realms—Superreality
- Finite manifestations of Infinity
- Partitioned consciousness
- Manifold-dimensioned (<12)
- Parallel Realms (a.k.a. planes)
- Existential superstructure
- Domain of mortality
- Finite Law Governance

Realm 666—Illusory Reality
- Tri-dimensioned (space-time-energy)
- Dominion of the First
- Exile of the Fallen Stars
- Domain of wo|man
- Entropic Governance

Eternity—Preterreality
- Eternal Void of origin and destination
- Singularity of consciousness
- Dimensionless
- Mathematic (or God forbid Chaotic) Governance

6.2 Down to Earth

When we first established COTC we put trainees straight into Red Phase and the washout rate was over 80 percent. The brutal conditions of extended duty in a finite environment, albeit simulated, proved overwhelming; thus, we instituted a period of orientation that now includes corporeal simulations. As a result, we have lowered our average course washout rate to just below 50 percent (contrary to what you may think, the Drill Seraphs value trainee retention over attrition).

The stresses of Red Phase stem, in large part, from submission to the laws of Finite Realm 666. For most of us

Finite Realm 666

separation is the most painful, gravity the most taxing, and tri-dimensional existentiality the most vexing.* In addition, these stresses are compounded by the debilitating effects of filth, consumption, and illness, owing to the baneful governance of Realm 666: Entropy.

The Divine Purge concluded the first campaign of the Civil War by separating loyal from rebel, pure from impure, enduring from entropic, Infinite from finite, and, most regrettably, mortal from Eternal. Within Realm 666, the 57th GSG watches over, protects, and influences assigned mortal charges to assist the Ghost of God preserve wo|men for return to the Infinite Dominion and, eventually, to the Eternal Void. Realm 666, of course, is the dominion of the First and his exiled minions—mastering their terrain strips them of one of the few advantages they have.

> The great dragon was hurled down–that ancient serpent called the devil, or Satan, who leads the whole world astray. He was hurled to the earth, and his angels with him. (Rev 12:9)
> Apostle Jyahn of Patmos

Your training will teach you practical techniques to endure and operate in the finite realms, and to prepare we believe a basic understanding of finite creation (Superreality), particularly as manifested in Realm 666 (Illusory Reality), is useful to the aspiring Earth Walker candidate.

First, it helps to recognize that the experiential basis of the 666th Finite Realm is tri-dimensional limitation: physical space, sequential time, and finite energy/matter into which nothing existential can be added.** The various components of a finite realm may change their nature, and constantly do, but the finite tri-dimensional sum total cannot be increased. In fact, with each rising of the sun, Realm 666 possesses slightly less space, time and energy (or matter) than under Earth's previous orbit. As the wisest DON observed, "there is nothing new under the Sun" (Eccl 1:9) and there never will be through Cessation when the 666th tapestry is rolled up and stored in the Temple of AΩ.

Until Cessation, we have access to this tapestry through the rhythmic weaving of the yarn of time. Time, the second dimension, paces the darning needle that regulates existential processes, notably ontogeny, within Illusory Reality. Naturally, we can only access DON through the current stitch in time, or what God the Founder has set aside as "today."

Today is the single darn of time that threads finite to Infinite. It is, therefore, the only Preservation opportunity, and yet, it is largely unrecognized by DON for she has a tendency to live in the past or in the future, which, by the flight, is another hallmark of the UTL.

> Because I could not stop for Death,
> He kindly stopped for me;
> The carriage held but just ourselves
> And Immortality[1]
>
> Emily Dickinson, poet,
> New Canaan, 656.720 to 677.174 AH

Regretting the past and fearing the future, certain men and women spend their ephemeral days out of reach and deaf to the call of the Eternal Ghost. For what is clear to you about finite existence is oft obscured to them; namely, yesterday and tomorrow, by definition, do not exist. Rather, they are Illusory Reality, stealing the awareness of our charges.

* Some argue that tying the laces of DON's footgear to be the most vexing! See www.557GSG.org for helpful hints on this subject.

** Mathematics, love, and Real-being incarnation breach the finite but so do without existential addition:

---

1. Dickinson, "The Chariot," 138.

- Under any governance save its own, mathematics is merely expression.
- Love elevates the mortal soul to Reality without existential impact.
- Spiritual incarnation, whether angelic or divine, utilizes available finite space-time-energy to incorporate a Real-being within Superreality.

6.3 About Time

Time is a physical construct necessary for the consistent application of both real and superreal laws for all events within a finite realm. While (or perhaps more accurately "not-while") finite time does not exist in Reality, it is a valid superreal figment in the same sense as space. Time plays a defining role for Superreality in that it modulates space-energy events to make them experientially coherent across all possible variations of artifact velocity and gravitational mass.

As you are starting to gather, finite time is unlike anything you have experienced in the Infinite and, as previously mentioned, its limitations are the cause of some Red Phase washouts. Understanding time in the abstract does diminish its ravaging impact upon your first time-submission experience. Describing the experience of time from the finite perspective to Real-beings accustomed to the dozen-dimensioned Infinite is difficult, but not impossible, if we challenge our imaginations.

So please imagine, if you will, that you shall compose and play a musical movement out of a limited supply of notes and chords; you must work within two octaves; there is only one key available to choose from; and the rhythm is inalterably syncopated.

It is that last limitation you will find particularly perturbing. If finite creation is a symphony, then time is its cadence, beating at precise intervals.* Now imagine that a maximum number of notes can be played between beats—not because it is pleasing to limit the notes, but because one simply cannot play more notes. Sounds incredible, does it not? Indeed, this oppressively linear advance of time bounds and defines mortal superreal and illusory experience, and it is the currency of human accomplishment.

What you know as Infinite Creation does, of course, exist across the finite realms as the substructure upon which Superreality overlays, but it is a rare DON indeed who recognizes this Reality and even rarer who corporeally enters the Infinite Dominion (e.g., Enoch, Seventh from Adam). In all but those rarest of cases, now is the only window we and the Ghost of God have to access DON, and in all cases now is the only opportunity for DON's Eternal Preservation.

> I tell you, now is the time of God's favor, now is the day of salvation. (2 Cor 6:2)
>
> Apostle Saul-Paul

Unfortunately, one of the more convincing spiritual lies, "When I die, God will save me from going to Hell," appeals to DON's spiritual naïveté. Earth Walker candidates will recognize this statement as an impossibility but we cannot overstate how pervasive and persuasive this peculiar prevarication is. Few wo|men come to recognize the Illusory Reality of the future and the uncomfortable fact that if they are not preserved during mortal life, they are lost forever.

> The greatest obstacle to living is expectancy, which hangs up tomorrow and loses today. You are arranging what lies in Fortune's control, and abandoning what lies in yours. What are

you looking at? To what goal are you straining? The whole future lies in uncertainty: live immediately.[2]
>Lucius Annaeus Seneca, philosopher,
>Palatine (GG), 717.351 AT to 12.053 AH

*Because time modulates space-energy events to be experientially coherent from the point of view of an artifact, a human being or incarnate Real-being will remain biologically unaware of time dilation regardless of differences in velocity and gravitational mass. In other words, time appears subjectively consistent even when its cadence is objectively relative.

6.4 Enoch's Time Piece

An effectual means to convey the experience of finite time to what you know in the dozen-dimensioned Dominion is "Enoch's Time Piece." Written by the mortal Enoch, 7th from Adam and 3rd fore Noah, at the behest of AA Gabriel, it is formally intended for Messenger Services. We find it useful for Guardian Services as well and invite you to "spend time" pondering its verses (sequentially of course).

.

---

2. Seneca, *Shortness of Life*, 13.

time, currency of mortal life
cartographer of physical events
doles, dimensions, and metes existence

time, warp and weft of the universe
picks and paces experience

time, breath of creation
hints evermore
confirms ever

now to now
life to death
water to spirit

obscuring eternity
yet revealing infinity
masterpiece of divinity

hallowed resurrection of today
illusion of tomorrow and yesterday

inestimable but calculable, what is this enigma
to mere mortal mind? For God only
knows what can part with time

6.5 Principal Existential Laws, 666th Superreal Plane

Critical to successful corporeal operations on Earth is awareness of how the Principal Existential Laws bound mortal experience, even that of the incarnate Logos, to tri-dimensional linear existence. More importantly, the Principal Existential Laws govern not only physical behavior but spiritual behaviors as well. As you will study in much greater detail during Academic Phase, the Principal Existential Laws are as follows.

Finite Realm 666

1. Inertia

A physical artifact at rest tends to stay at rest; a physical artifact in motion tends to stay in motion. This also applies to DON's spiritual life momentums (see Appendix 10: AA Raphael's Spiritual Assessment Matrix [SPAM]). At rest, a.k.a. unborn, DON is spiritually immobilized and the tendency to remain at rest yields bounties for the First and oft frustrates the combined efforts of the Host and Ghost. As noted in the first chapters of Section 4, unborn DON accepts the illusory reality manipulated by the fallen First Archlumen as truth, and she can be quite intractable despite our best efforts to show her otherwise.

> The god of this age has blinded the minds of unbelievers, so that they cannot see the light of the gospel that displays the glory of Christ, who is the image of God. (2 Cor 4:4)
>
> Apostle Saul-Paul

With prayer, persistence, and perseverance, however, we can penetrate the veil of darkness and persuade a precious few to follow the light, whence they will move along the spiritual continuum continuously. Which direction they travel, though, is our constant concern given the second Principal Existential Law: Reaction.

2. Reaction

For every action there is a corresponding equal and opposite reaction. Physically speaking this is a rather benign consequential constant. Spiritually, on the other wing, it keeps us ever vigilant and active. DON tends to believe her spiritual path is single mode: forward from birth. She may think she stops at points along the way or veers off trajectory but assumes that overall she hurtles forward from her original spiritual launch. In Reality she bounds bi-directionally—either toward or away from God the Founder. The tenacious assault of the Insurrection and the headwinds of Entropy will reverse her course if she does not continuously power the engine of her life momentum: her faith. With God's Eternal Ghost we do everything we can to assist, but ultimately DON must renew her faith daily, tapping the Abundant Wellspring of Life.

3. Sequentialism

Finite existence can only be experienced in chronological series, as neither full dozen-dimensional access nor experiential time division* is possible. Spiritually speaking, this requires DON to prioritize her finite space-time-energy.

While Entropy, monstrous offspring of the Civil War, rails simultaneously against the entire composition of mortal life, DON must choose which element of her life to rebuild first, then second, then third, and before long she must return to the first lest it succumb to Entropy's relentless assault.

Sequentialism necessarily leaves many elements of DON's composite existence in disarray. As discussed in chapter 2.3, the hazard is DON may choose unwisely, preferring the temporal over the Infinite, Mammon over Jyeshua, life over Life. Examine a charge's expenditure of finite space-time-energy and you will quickly learn what she values and, furthermore, where you may need to redirect her attentions.

4. Gravity

Physically speaking, the mutual attraction of physical bodies governs and balances finite space-time-energy within the visible universe of the 666th Plane. You will immediately find the physical pull of Gravity to be exhausting and you may, therefore, assume it a bane, but it is the necessary governance of what would otherwise be an unmanageably imbalanced finite creation.

The gift of Gravity, balance, also forms the fundamental logic of superreal existence from the act of walking, to criminal law, to the sacrifice of Jyeshua. Encoded into every wo|man's deoxyribonucleic acid, regardless of mental disease or emotional defect, is the gravitational assumption that the scales should be balanced (if only as applicable to herself). Thus we observe universal demands for equity, belief in fairness, and social compacts supported by retribution-based justice systems (an eye for an eye).

5. Spatial, Chronological, and Modulatory (SCM) Separation

The limitations imposed by tri-dimensional Superreality separate the finite into discreet existentialities; therefore, an artifact is directly influenced only by present (proximately immediate and temporally concurrent) energy (or its variant matter). Stated inversely, non-local causation is not possible within Superreality.** Accordingly, for COs to operate within a finite realm, we must abide by discreetly dimensioned space-time-energy, which includes partitioning angelic consciousness individually. This presents quite a challenge because partitioned consciousness prohibits sentient access to the substructural switching fabric, the medium of non-local connection in Finite Realm 666.

Without a non-local connection, the only bridge to the Infinite Dominion wo|men and deployed Earth Walkers have is local intercourse (communion), save for those rarified human masters of meditation, mostly appearing in and around Center Earth and India.*** Ergo, the deployed CO is spiritually incommunicado.

This is an exceptionally exigent state for even the strongest among us to endure. In fact, some of us succumb to separation anxiety, abandonment syndrome, and Fictional-Existence Stress Disorder (FESD). Frequently fretful, forlorn, and fatigued, Red Phase candidates often washout due to the stress of corporeal training and, in rare cases, the stress of extended corporeal operations has led to angelic psychosis (which AA Raphael's Spirysicians can treat and cure).

The foremost distressing aspect of SCM Separation is that Earth Walkers cease to exist in any Real sense during finite deployments, owing to the Fourth Principal Law's Ontological Principle. Just as mortals do not exist except during temporary and sporadic experiences of communion built upon the inconvenient and unstable causeway of local intercourse (be it with other human-beings or Real-beings), so it goes with COs.

> The objects of sense exist only when they are perceived; the trees therefore are in the garden, or the chairs in the parlour, no longer than while there is somebody by to perceive them.[3]
> George Berkeley, cleric and philosopher,
> Hreyisles (GG), 603.758 to 628.595 AH

The Fourth Principal Law's Ontological Principle states that mortals Really exist only in interaction. By way of explanation, remember that tri-dimensioned Superreality is merely a superstructure built upon the Real substructure of dozen-dimensioned Infinity. These two orders of reality meet at the substructural switching fabric wherein Superreality and Reality coexist but Reality does so only as probabilities, manifesting as observable and partially

---

3. Berkeley, *Treatise*, sec. 45.

measureable Superreality only upon interaction with a superreal figment. Moreover, Real probabilities also manifest as observable and partially measurable Reality upon interaction with a Real component and this has significant implications for DON's spiritual (a.k.a. Real) existence.

Specifically, DON's spiritual state (see Appendix 9: Calculating the Probability of Preservation, and Appendix 10: AA Raphael's Spiritual Assessment Matrix [SPAM]) exists only as a probability within Superreality until she interacts with Reality. As we mentioned in 2.5: Communion, DON can transcend temporal Illusory Reality into Infinite Reality via communion (spiritual interaction) with one another, communion with creation, and communion with Real-beings, for such are the gateways to the Dominion. These Reality-transcending interactions, therefore, define wo|man's Real existence, or, as the complete quotation from AA Raphael goes, "apart from communion, DON is naught, and though she ought, DON is not distraught, because toward this truth she gives no thought."

6. Entropy

Finite existence, including that of a spiritual nature, tends toward disorganization and disintegration. The end-state of Entropy is chaos, toward which the Insurrection of the First ardently pushes in the belief that complete chaos will trigger the Apocalypse on terms favorable to the Insurrection (such an event could very well be deleterious for all, but he who has nothing to lose is willing to take his chances).

> Based on the assumption of a 'closed' universe . . . the second law of thermodynamics prescribes an inexorable move towards ever higher

> entropy, disorder. Chaos wins! . . . Against this I claim that we live in an open universe, because God continues his creative work until on the last Day he will completely abolish remaining chaos and perfect his universe without letting it go to complete decay.[4]
>
> Sjoerd Bonting, alchemist,
> Greater Gothika, 691.053 to ExTBA AH

As we will describe in the next chapter dedicated to this subject, while we have concern regarding the chaotic aims of the Adversary, we are primarily concerned about Entropy's relentless assault on the spiritual health of our charges.

* DON does communicate via approximate forms of time division, such as electromagnetic signal multiplexing and light frequency division multiplexing.

** Excluding through the substructural switching fabric, which DON calls the quantum or subatomic level.

*** This edition of *Bound* naturally focuses on the cultural, philosophical, and religious forces that have influenced the development of New Canaanite society; for information on other Thrones such as Center Earth and India, consult the applicable handbook edition.

6.6 Entropy

Within the 666th Finite Realm, harnessed energy tends to dissipate; organization tends to disorganize. The Descendants of Noah readily grasp this concept as it applies to the physical world they are presently confined to. For example, you will observe them curing meats, staining wood, cleaning dwellings, and, odd though it is, preserving corpses. Despite their attentions to the physical body after life, when

---

4. Bonting, *God's Action*, 397.

Finite Realm 666

it comes to Entropy of the living body, you will likely assess their awareness to be less than optimal.

Naturally you will observe DON's regular consumption of organic nourishment and the restoration of energy through sleep, but most other anti-entropic activities receive far less regular attention, such as exercise, relaxation, and, a personal favorite of ours, the never sufficiently frequent brushing of teeth (you'll understand what we mean when you take your first corporeal assignment).

Spawn on the Fall, Entropy is an indefatigable ally of the First against wo|man. Left unfettered, we postulate it possesses the potential to collapse the finite plane of Realm 666 into chaos; the corollary results of which are conjecture and the subject of much learned debate, but we can be assume such an outcome would destabilize the 666th Realm, possibly all Superreality, and perhaps even the Infinite Dominion herself.

> The entropy of the universe tends to a maximum.[5]
> Rudolf Clausius, alchemist,
> Greater Gothika, 653.798 to 677.904 AH

The standard supposition states that if Entropy collapses one realm into chaos, it will trigger a chain reaction culminating in a comprehensive collapse of Creation: all planes, all planets, all peoples (innocent and fallen alike). A less accepted hypothesis, but certainly one the First believes, is that the collapse of Superreality would coincidentally unravel its Real substructure and the contiguous Infinite Dominion with it, and thereby usher a premature return to the Void under the Governance of Chaos, which would exclude all that is Holy. While most of us doubt this outcome is possible we do not dismiss Entropy's potential hazards at least to our charges and we therefore battle its relentless assault at

---

5. Clausius, *Mechanical Theory*, 365.

every turn. For the Earth Walker, this means awakening our charges and inspiring them toward order.

This brings us to the most important agency of Entropy as it relates to mortals, which is over the health of souls trapped in the finite creation. Here, we are sad to say, we find little human understanding and even less application.

In short, the Descendants of Noah are predisposed to the false notion that their spiritual lives do not require maintenance. Widespread denial of their spirituality notwithstanding, the few who gain faith and come into personal communion with the Founder, Ghost & Logos, are apt to neglect those relationships, and, therefore, their spiritual health.

The reasons for humanity's reluctance to acknowledge the law of Spiritual Entropy are multifarious but it is predominantly due to the concerted efforts of the Insurrection of the First. Given the transmogrified nature of both fallen beings, a demon is far more effective in communicating to DON than angels are. They both speak languages, greed and lust for example, that we simply do not comprehend.

If you can impress upon your charges the constant threat Entropy poses to their spiritual livelihoods, and, more importantly, the practical methods to combat it, you will have done well. The Descendant of Noah who spends first daylight in prayer, gives thanks throughout the day, fellowships, renders aid, learns from elders, teaches youth, and provides for widows and orphans draws from the Abundant Wellspring of Life and does not suffer spiritual decay. Those who neglect their spiritual health, however, risk slipping back into the mesmerizing control of the enemy.

You will likely find this fight exhausting but, given the gravity of the potential outcome, we must all constantly battle the forces of Entropy in order to not only preserve DON but, perhaps, even ourselves.

Section 7

Appendices

Appendix 1: Organizational Chart, 57th GSB

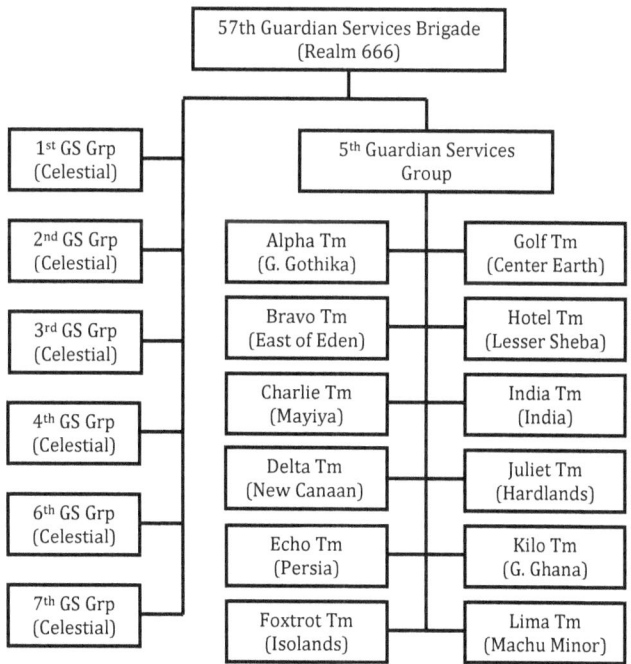

Appendix 2: Chain of Command, Delta Team, 5/57 GSG, 7th Holy Legion

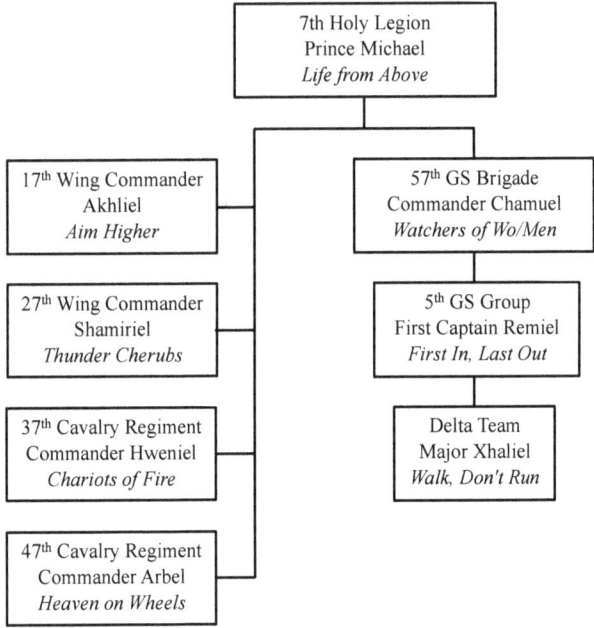

Appendices

Appendix 3: Mission Statement, Delta Team, 5/57 GSG

The mission of Delta Team, 5/57 Guardian Service Group is to watch over the Descendants of Noah in the New Canaan AOR during the Age of Harvest through covert, corporeal interdiction and reconnaissance, and through covert combat operations support, in order to aid the Ghost of God to preserve the Descendants of Noah.

Mission Amplification

The two primary mission tasks of Corporeal Operatives are interdiction and reconnaissance. COs interdict spiritual false practices by supplanting spiritual counterfeit with spiritual truth and by implementing countermeasures to personal rebellions. COs also reconnoiter behind enemy lines to garner information generally imperceptible from the Infinite Dominion, such as impact of Insurrection efforts on human politics, religious movements, cultural currents, and emotional, physical, and psychological health at both the individual and social levels. Through liaison with Winged Operatives (WOs), COs provide Active Lies, Propagation, Enemy Order of Battle, and Surroundings Reports (APESREP) to 5th GSG R&S for analysis, interpretation, and dissemination.

A secondary mission task of the CO is to conduct covert combat operations support. During Holy Legion conventional combat operations, COs serve as forward observers (FOs), providing reports on demonic maneuvers and effectiveness of Holy Legion indirect fires via encoded linear communications to a Superreal Tactical Entry Point (STEP) site.

Appendix 4: Higher Organizational Mission Statements

The mission of the Army of the Lord is to neutralize insurgent spiritual forces in the finite realms until Cessation through direct and indirect combat operations in order to aid the Ghost of God preserve mortal souls and prepare the Dominion for return to the Eternal Void.

The mission of the 7th Holy Legion is to neutralize the Insurrection of the First in Finite Realm 666 until Cessation through direct and indirect combat operations in order to aid the Ghost of God preserve the Descendant's of Noah and prepare Theatre 666 for return to the Dominion.

The mission of the 57th Guardian Service Brigade is to watch over the Descendants of Noah on Earth, Realm 666, until End Times through covert spiritual over-watch and intervention, covert corporeal reconnaissance and influence, and combat operations support, in order to aid the Ghost of God preserve the Descendants of Noah.

The mission of the 5th Guardian Service Group/57th Guardian Service Brigade is to watch over the Descendants of Noah on Earth, Realm 666, until End Times through covert corporeal interdiction and reconnaissance, and through covert combat operations support, in order to aid the Ghost of God preserve the Descendants of Noah.

> The Lord will watch over your coming and going both now and forevermore. (Ps 121:8)
> *Tehillim*

Appendices

Appendix 5: Standing Orders, Earth Walkers, 5/57 GSG

1. I will obey the lawful orders of those appointed over me.

2. I will serve the Descendants of Noah with all my spirit.

3. I will not reveal my angelic nature to a mortal except on the order of Archangel Gabriel, Minister of Communications, 7th District of the Dominion.

4. I will guard my charge and quit my charge only when properly relieved.

5. I will not directly engage insurgent demonic forces save for the following circumstances:

   A. Demonic forces detect and assault a GS operative with overwhelming force.

   B. A DON marked by D-F&D as PC1 faces imminent peril with eternal consequences.

Appendix 6: Order of Battle, 6th Unholy Legion

6th Unholy Legion
Master & Commander: First Archlumen

6th Legion Strategem Staff
Insurrection Executive Officer: Commodore Beelzebub

First Sworn Subjects (FSS)
Chief: Grand Marshal Baal

60th Naught Fleet
Commander: Vice Admiral Leviathan

61st Subterranean Reconnaissance Unit
Commander: Rear Admiral Bal'am

62nd Demonic Wing
Commander: Flight Marshal Belial

64th Demonic Wing
Commander: Flight Marshal Wormwood

65th Armored Nephilim Division
Commander: Field Marshal Gog

66th Armored Nephilim Division
Commander: Field Marshal Magog

68th Security Forces, *Hades Hellions*
Commander: Marshal Abaddon

69th Black Ops Operatives (*BOO!*)
Commander: Marshal Mammon

Appendix 7: COTC Phases

Candidates who successfully graduate COTC will complete the following phases.

Orientation Phase

Goal: Prepare candidates to enter COTC Red Phase
Means: Partial corporeal manifestation and physical conditioning
Standard: 77% or higher on all physical fitness tests

Appendices

Red Phase

Goal: Select candidates capable of long-term operations in finite realms
Means: Immersion in virtual Finite Realm 666 environments
Standard: Go/No-Go

Academic Phase

Goal: Master information pertinent to corporeal operations
Means: Instruction and study
Standard: 77% or higher comprehension rate on all examinations

Orange Phase

Goal: Learn and apply counter insurgency tactics
Means: Study and virtual training
Standard: Pass 77% of training exercises first attempt, remainder second attempt

Blue Phase

Goal: Learn and apply human intervention methodologies
Means: Study and virtual training
Standard: Pass 77% of training exercises first attempt, remainder second attempt

Green Phase

Goal: Integrate previous phase learning to validate deployment readiness

Means: Virtual training and supervised earth deployment practicum
Standard: Go/No-Go

Appendix 8: Charge Alarm Signals

When a charge demonstrates behavior matching several of the following alarm signals, her faith is slipping and the enemy is rapidly gaining ground. Immediate intervention on our part is of utmost urgency.

- *Bored with God.* Unmotivated to keep her relationship with God active. Would rather do nothing than fellowship or pray. Makes excuses why other concerns in her life come before God. Prefers worldly pursuits over spiritual ones.

- *Blaming.* Blames everyone else for her own mistakes and faults.

- *Restless.* Becomes constantly agitated; always in motion yet never moving forward; she can neither sit still nor progress.

- *Chronically Ill.* Chronically suffers physical illness directly related to stress and anxiety.

- *All-Knowing.* She does not need anyone else's input but others need and will be told hers. No one can tell her anything. She knows all she needs to know and if there is something she does not know, then it obviously is not worth knowing.

- *Mean-Spirited.* She repeatedly hurts those around her, especially those she loves the most. She abuses others: spouse, child, friend, coworker, pet, etc.

- *Greedy.* Never satisfied, she worships the root of all evil: the love of more.*

Appendices

- *Lazy.* Your charge slows her spiritual walk. She starts waking up later and praying less. She stops reading Scripture every day. She skips a few fellowship meetings. She decides not to call an accountability partner—again.
- *Persecution Complex.* "Why me? Why, why, why?! It's not fair!!"
- *Hypersensitive.* She often interprets benign or unrelated comments to be indictments of her character and conduct.
- *Arrogant.* She is a saint in her own eyes. She is royalty and others are serfs.
- *Entitled.* Everyone owes her special treatment just for being who she is. She does not need to earn—simply her presence is sufficient.
- *Excessively Medicating.* She abuses alcohol and/or prescription medicine, and/or she uses narcotics.
- *Irritable.* Everything annoys her. "It's too loud; it's too quiet. It's too warm; it's too cold. My wife won't shut up; my husband won't open up. The phone rings all the time; no one ever calls me."
- *Volatile.* She is prone to unrestrained outbursts of childish fury known as temper tantrums, which usually include physical demonstrations such as throwing semi-valuable items, punching solid surfaces, and kicking immovable objects (sadly, this is neither an uncommon behavior nor an exaggerated description).
- *Despairing.* She feels all is lost, all is hopeless, all is forlorn.
- *Deceiving.* She deceives others and herself of the truth regarding her behaviors.

- *Secretive.* She keeps secrets about herself from everyone in her life (note: your charge's spiritual illness can be measured by the depth and quantity of her secrets).

* DON sometimes misunderstands extent scriptures to state that the love of money is the root of all evil; whereas money plays quite the opposite role in modern society, or as Ayn Rand, author, New Canaan, 684.113 to 712.238 AH, said, "Until and unless you discover that money is the root of all good, you ask for your own destruction. When money ceases to become the means by which men deal with one another, then men become the tools of other men. Blood, whips and guns—or dollars. Take your choice—there is no other."[1]

Appendix 9: Calculating the Probability of Preservation

DON's spiritual state (the intersection of finite life momentum and infinite spiritual position) exists only as a probability within the Superreality of the finite creation. Specifically, the more precisely we determine the life momentum of DON, the less precisely we can determine her spiritual position, and vice versa. Fortunately, we can calcuate fairly reliable probabilities utilizing AA Raphael's Spiritual Assessment Matrix (SPAM).

Depicted in Appendix 10, AA Raphael's SPAM enables you to locate DON's critical spiritual momentums between two poles representative of spiritual death and Preservation, and then correlates those momentums to the seven phases of human spiritual development. Considering a charge's spiritual momentums in light of the possible phases of development within the SPAM matrix will narrow a charge's potential spiritual position to a few possibilities. You will

---

1. Rand, *Atlas Shrugged*, 385.

Appendices

then have to apply your knowledge of your charge and the larger context in which she acts to reckon what phase she is likely in for each spiritual momentum evaluated. Once you complete the matrix you can then populate values into the Preservation Probability formulae shown below to calculate the probability she is preserved, a.k.a. "saved."*

> Where P(P) is the Preservation Probability:
> $\{α1ω1:α3ω17\}`55 \ldots χ$
> $\{αhω1: αhω21\}`133 \ldots φ$
> $\{α4ω1:α7ω21\}`150 \ldots ψ$
> $P(P) \ldots χ|ψ\text{-}φ$

Note: negative probabilities indicate probability of eternal loss.

 * Postmortem data validate the SPAM is accurate when utilized by Guardians with one or more eras of corporeal experience (far less accurate, of course, when utilized by callow operatives).

Bound, an Earth Walker's Handbook

Appendix 10: AA Raphael's Spiritual Assessment Matrix (SPAM)

↓Spiritual Momentum ω	Unborn	Gestation	Labor	Birth	Premature Death	Infancy	Childhood	Adolescence	Maturity	
1 Isolation	I	IC	IC	C	I	IC	IC	IC	IC	Connection
2 Blindness	B	B	B	BS	BS	BS	BS	S	S	Sight
3 Dormant	D	D	D	A	A	A	A	A	A	Awake
4 Captivity	C	CF	CF	F	C	F	CF	CF	CF	Freedom
5 Unconscious	U	U	U	C	U	C	C	C	C	Conscious
6 Unaware	U	U	U	UA	UA	UA	UA	UA	A	Aware
7 Unreality	U	U	UR	R	U	R	R	UR	R	Reality
8 Drifting	n/a	n/a	n/a	n/a	D	DS	DS	DS	DS	Seeking
9 Disingenuous	D	DS	DS	DS	D	S	S	DS	S	Sincere
10 Self-reliant	S	SG	SG	SG	S	SG	SG	SG	SG	Ghost-reliant
11 Self-centric	SO	SO	SO	SO	SO	S	SO	SO	SO	Other-centric
12 Hubris	Hb	HbHm	HbHm	HbHm	HbHm	HbHm	HbHm	HbHm	Hm	Humility
13 Secrets	S	SN	SN	SN	SN	N	N	N	SN	No secrets
14 My will	M	M	M	T	M	MT	MT	MT	T	Thy will
15 Do	DB	DB	DB	DB	DoBe	DB	DB	DB	B	Be
16 Control	CR	C	CR	CR	CR	R	CR	CR	R	Release
17 Suspect	S	S	ST	T	S	T	ST	ST	ST	Trust
18 Rebellious	n/a	n/a	n/a	n/a	R	A	RA	RA	A	Allegiant
19 Denial	n/a	n/a	n/a	n/a	D	DA	DA	DA	DA	Admission
20 Acquiesced	n/a	n/a	n/a	n/a	A	V	V	AV	AV	Victorious
21 Falling	n/a	n/a	n/a	n/a	F	C	FC	FC	C	Climbing

		Spoilt ←———— Spiritual State Probability Continuum ————→ *Preserved*								
	Null	**Dead**								**Alive**
Spiritual Phase α	0	1	2	3	h	4	5	6	7	
		Groaning Ghost				Founder, Ghost, Logos				
		Jyeshua Introduced			UTL	GS Counter Insurgency				
Law Introduced		Spiritual Counterfeit								Grace

Appendices

Appendix 11: Martial Prerequisites

Heavenly Host Basic Training (H2BT)
Army of the Lord Advanced Training (AOLAT)
Completion of three Tours of Duty in the AOL or MS
Guardian Services Selection Course (GSSC)
Guardian Services Operations School (GSOS)

1. GSOS I: GS Fundamentals
2. GSOS II: Individual Training and Practicum
3. GSOS III: Unit Training

Completion of one Tour of Duty in a 57th GSB Celestial Group
Completion of the Corporeal Warfare Course
Completion of the following Specialized Skills Schools (S3):

1. Demonic Captivity Survival
2. Demonic Interception & Interdiction
3. Demonic Arrest & Detainment
4. Escape & Evasion
5. Finite Extraction
6. Finite Healing
7. Finite Jump School

Appendix 12: Media Prerequisites

A. Angels
   1. Billy Graham, *Angels*
   2. Frank Capra, *It's a Wonderful Life*
   3. Frank Peretti, *This Present Darkness* and *Piercing the Darkness*

B. Blindness
   1. Hans Christian Anderson, *The Emperor's New Clothes*
   2. John Newton, "Amazing Grace"
   3. Charles S. Stone, *American Pharisee*

C. Courage
   1. George Stevens Jr., *Thurgood*
   2. Gus Lee, *China Boy*
   3. Kimberly Peirce and Andy Bienen, *Boys Don't Cry*

D. DON's Psyche
   1. William Shakespeare, *The Complete Collection*
   2. www.facebook.com
   3. King World, *The Oprah Winfrey Show* (all episodes)

E. Earth
   1. Frtijof Capra, *The Tao of Physics*
   2. National Geographic Society, *National Geographic* (all issues)
   3. Steven Hawking, *A Brief History of Time*
   4. Pearl S. Buck, *The Good Earth*
   5. Carl Sagan, *Cosmos* (all episodes)
   6. Gary Zukav, *Dancing Wu Li Masters*

Appendices

F. Fellowship of Suffering
   1. Alcoholics Anonymous, *Alcoholics Anonymous*
   2. John Steinbeck, *Grapes of Wrath*
   3. Macy Gray, "Still"

G. God
   1. Bruce Feiler, *Abraham*
   2. Josh McDowell, *More than a Carpenter*
   3. Vine Deloria Jr., *God Is Red*

H. History of contemporary New Canaan
   1. Alex Haley, *Roots* (TV miniseries)
   2. PBS, *Ancestors in the Americas* (TV documentary)
   3. *New York Times* (all issues)

I. Injustice
   1. Harper Lee, *To Kill a Mockingbird*
   2. Dee Alexander Brown, *Bury My Heart at Wounded Knee*
   3. Cat in the Hat Productions, *How the Grinch Stole Christmas!*

J. Judicial
   1. Genna Rae McNeil, *Ground Work: Charles Hamilton Houston and the Struggle for Civil Rights*
   2. Jerome Lawrence and Robert E. Lee, *Inherit the Wind*
   3. United States Supreme Court, all cases, all opinions.

K. Kryptonite
   1. Stephen Frears and Christopher Hampton, *Dangerous Liaisons* (1988)
   2. Oliver Stone, *Wall Street*
   3. David Sheff, *Beautiful Boy*

Bound, an Earth Walker's Handbook

L. Love

1. Stephen E. Ambrose, *Band of Brothers*
2. Christopher Reeve and Alice Elliot Dark, *In the Gloaming*
3. Jonathon Larson, *Rent*

M. Misery

1. Alice Walker, *The Color Purple*
2. Tim McGraw, *Let It Go*
3. Dante Alighieri, *Inferno*

N. Nobility

1. Kathryn Spink, *Mother Teresa*
2. Stephen Spielberg and Stephen Zaillian, *Schindler's List*
3. Stanley Vestal, *Sitting Bull, Champion of the Sioux*

O. Out of Illusory Reality

1. Andy and Lana Wachowski, *The Matrix*
2. Plato, *Allegory of the Cave*
3. Patrick Carnes, *Out of the Shadows*

P. Politics

1. Thomas Paine, *Common Sense*
2. Niccolo Machievelli, *The Prince*
3. Economist Newspaper Limited, *The Economist* (all issues)

Q. Quill

1. Emily Dickinson, *The Poems of Emily Dickinson*
2. Willa Cather, *My Ántonia*
3. Toni Morrison, *Beloved*

R. Reason

1. Marcus Aurelius, *Meditations*

Appendices

- 2. Donald Kalish, Richard Montague, and Gary Mar, *Logic: Techniques of Formal Reasoning* (2nd ed.)
- 3. Robert Fulghum, *All I Really Need to Know I Learned in Kindergarten*

S. Spiritual Development

- 1. Helene and Powell Royster, eds., *Unquiet Pilgrimage: Journal of Robert Stewart Royster*
- 2. C. S. Lewis, *Pilgrim's Regress*
- 3. David McCasland, *Oswald Chambers: Abandoned to God*

T. Typecasts of DON

- 1. Benjamin Hoff, *The Tao of Pooh*
- 2. Paul Haggis, *Crash*
- 3. Gene Roddenberry, *Star Trek: The Original Series*

U. Undertow

- 1. Andrew Solomon, *The Noonday Demon*
- 2. Sylvia Plath, *The Bell Jar*
- 3. Francis Ford Coppola, *Apocalypse Now*

V. Victimization

- 1. Theda Perdue and Michael D. Green, *The Cherokee Nation and the Trail of Tears*
- 2. Laurie Hall, *An Affair of the Mind*
- 3. Bob Dylan, "The Hurricane"

W. Women

- 1. Christine de Pizan, *The Book of the City of Ladies*
- 2. Mary Wollstonecraft, *A Vindication of the Rights of Woman*
- 3. James Duff, *The Closer* (all episodes)

Bibliography

Adams, Charles Francis, editor. *Familial Letters of John Adams and His Wife Abigail Adams, during the Revolution*. New York: Hurd and Houghton, 1876.

Aquinas, Thomas. *Summa Theologica*. Part II-II (Secunda-Secundae). New York: Benziger, 2006.

Beauvoir, Simone de. *The Ethics of Ambiguity*. Translated by Bernard Frechtman. New York: Citadel, 1948.

Berkeley, George. *Treatise Concerning the Principles of Human Knowledge*. Dublin: Jeremy Pepyat, 1710.

Berra, Yogi. *The Yogi Book: I Really Didn't Say Everything I Said!*. New York: Workman, 2010.

Bonting, Sjoerd. "God's Action in the World: Influencing of Chaos Events?" *Sewanee Theological Review*. 47 (September 2004), 372–401.

Book of Enoch the Prophet. Translated by Richard Laurence. London: W. Clowes & Sons, 1883.

Burns, Alexander. "How Much Do Voters Know?" *Politico*, March 2012. Online: http://www.politico.com/news/stories/0312/73947.html.

Chambers, Oswald. *My Utmost for His Highest*. London: Dodd, Mead, 1935.

Clausius, Rudolf. *The Mechanical Theory of Heat, with Its Application to the Steam-Engine and to the Physical Properties of Bodies*. London: John Van Voorst, 1867.

Covey, Steven, R. *The Seven Habits of Highly Effective People: Restoring the Character Ethic*. New York: Free Press, 1989.

Dickinson, Emily. "The Chariot." In *Poems*, edited by Mabel Loomis Todd and T. W. Higginson, 138–39. 11th ed. Boston: Roberts Brothers, 1890.

Bibliography

Emerson, Ralph Waldo. "Self-Reliance." In *The Works of Ralph Waldo Emerson: Essays, First Series*. New York: Houghton, Mifflin, 1883 [1841].

Galilei, Galileo. "Letter to the Grand Duchess Christina." In *Discoveries and Opinions of Galileo*. Translated by Stillman Drake. New York: Doubleday, 1957.

Hazlitt, William. "On the Spirit of Monarchy." In *Literary Remains of the Late William Hazlitt*. London: Saunders & Otley, 1836.

Kempis, á Thomas. *The Imitation of Christ*. Revised translation edited by Hal M. Helms and Robert J. Edmonson. Brewster, MA: Paraclete, 2008.

King, Martin Luther, Jr. "Remaining Awake through a Great Revolution, Commencement Address." *Oberlin Alumni Magazine* (August 1965), 4–9. Online: http://www.thekingcenter.org/archive/document/oberlin-college-commencement#.

Lewis, C. S. *The Screwtape Letters*. New York: Touchstone, 1996.

Ma, Yo-Yo. "The Big Interview: Yo-Yo Ma pays back his debt to Toronto." *Toronto.com*, May 25, 2012. Online: http://www.toronto.com/article/729611.

Marcus Aurelius. *Meditations*. Radford: Wilder, 2008.

Pizan, Christine de. *The Book of the City of Ladies*. Translated by Earl Jeffrey Richards. New York: Persea, 1982.

Rand, Ayn. *Atlas Shrugged*. New York: SIGNET, 1957.

Raymond, Rossiter W. "Immortal Love." In *Christus Consolator, and Other Poems*. New York: Thomas Y. Crowell Co., 1916.

Roosevelt, Eleanor. *You Learn by Living: Eleven Keys for a More Fulfilling Life*. New York: Harper & Row, 1960.

Russell, Bertrand. "Why I Am Not a Christian." In *Why I Am Not a Christian, and Other Essays on Religion and Related Subjects*. New York: Touchstone, 1957.

Seneca. *On the Shortness of Life*. Translated by C.D.N. Costa. New York: Penguin, 2005.

Sotomayor, Sonia. "Supreme Court Justice Sonia Sotomayor Addresses NYU Commencement." *NYU School of Law New,* May 18, 2012. Online: http://www.law.nyu.edu/news/SOTOMAYOR_SONIA_COMMENCEMENT_2012.

Stark, Thom. *The Human Faces of God: What Scripture Reveals When It Gets God Wrong (and Why Inerrancy Tries to Hide It)*. Eugene: Wipf & Stock, 2011.

Wachowski, Andy, and Larry Wachowski. *The Matrix: The Shooting Script*. New York: Newmarket, 2001.

Bibliography

Wordsworth, William. "Inscription in and near a Hermit's Cell." In *The Complete Poetical Works of William Wordsworth*. New York: Thomas Y. Crowell Co., 1892.

www.ingramcontent.com/pod-product-compliance
Lightning Source LLC
Chambersburg PA
CBHW071440160426
43195CB00013B/1980